Samurai Armies of the Late Sengoku Period

Volume I
Anatomy of a Samurai Army in the 16th and 17th Centuries

Till Weber

Dai ichi, dai man, dai kichi
"Great victory, long life, much happiness"

Motto used on his heraldic devices by Ishida Mitsunari, the great loser of the decisive battle of Sekigahara in 1600.

Author & translator: Till Weber
Illustrations: Rolf Fuhrmann / Sascha Lunyakov

Publisher: Zeughaus Verlag GmbH
Knesebeckstr. 88
10623 Berlin, Germany
Telephone: +49 (0)30/315 700 30
Email: info@zeughausverlag.de
Website: www.zeughausverlag.de

All rights reserved.
Reproduction, translation and photographic reproduction, including extracts are forbidden. Storage and distribution including transfer onto electronic media like CD-ROM etc. as well as storage on electronic media like the Internet etc. are not permissible without the express written permission of the publisher and are punishable.
Bibliographic information from the Deutschen Bibliothek: The Deutsche Bibliothek lists this publication in the German National Bibliography; detailed bibliographic information is available at http://dnb.ddb.de

Printed in European Union

Originally published in German as *"Die Samurai der Sengoku-Zeit. Band 1"*. Heere & Waffen Series, 9. (Berlin: Zeughaus Verlag, 2009) Revised and augmented English edition.

© 2022 Zeughaus Verlag GmbH, Berlin, Germany
ISBN: 978-3-96360-041-8

CONTENTS

Author's note	9
Periods of Japanese History	10
Basics of Japanese Military History c. 1600	12
Arms and Armour	14
Samurai	14
Ashigaru	29
Composition and Command Structure of a Samurai Army	35
Lord, Family, and Vassals	35
Command Structure	35
Feudal Samurai Service and Professional Troops in Garrisons	41
Strength and Composition of Armies	42
Army Divisions and Troop Types	45
Samurai Cavalry: Myth and Reality – The Takeda Re-Examined	45
Infantry I: Specialists with polearms	58
Infantry II: Missile Troops (Bow and Arquebus)	59
Honjin – The Headquarters Unit	63
Supply and Baggage Train	74
Samurai as Mercenaries	75
A Samurai Army in Action	77
On the March	77
In Camp	82
In Battle – Sengoku Period Tactics	88
A Standard Basic Unit Reconstructed	94
Key Terms in Japanese and English	100
Bibliography	101

AUTHOR'S NOTE

While there are a number of good studies of samurai-related topics in Western languages, detailed analysis of the structure and efficiency of a samurai army at its peak in the late 16th and early 17th century has been relatively scarce. This book tries to examine the body of a samurai army and reveal its inner workings as well as explain its outer appearance. How was it raised and maintained, what hierarchies and structures gave it coherence, what were its strengths and weaknesses? How did men specializing in different weapons and techniques fight as a cohesive unit and what were the differences compared to European armies? Towards the end of our period, armies could exceed the size of 100,000 men – How was this mass controlled using pre-modern means of communication? What was the role of fortifications, firearms and heraldic devices? We will be looking at tactics, marching and fighting formations and camp customs, sketching out both the great picture and numerous minor details by analyzing units down to a man. We will meet samurai in dramatic situations and look at the wonderful world of their arms and armour, at their horses and battle flags and much more.

Many terms and ideas are not widely familiar to the Western reader, not least Japanese words. Important concepts will be carefully explained using both the English language and a wealth of illustrations, many of them specially commissioned for this book, and photographs taken by the author during his 25 years in Japan. The basis for this book is drawn from Japanese primary sources, both textual and pictorial, and secondary works in Japanese, English, and other languages. This book first appeared in German as one of two volumes at Zeughaus Verlag, Berlin. Both have been translated into English by the author, and also carefully revised and augmented.

The author is deeply indebted for precious cooperation to Prof Masuo Kataoka (formerly of the University of the Ryukyus), Werner David, Hans-Dieter Oldhafer, Louise Williams, John Cruikshank, Rod Johnson, Thomas Körner, Stefan Müller and his team at Zeughaus Verlag, and last but not least my wife Sumie Ishii-Weber.

As for rendering Japanese words in Latin characters: For ease of reading, no macrons are used. Family names generally come before personal names.

Till Weber
Okinawa, March 2022

PERIODS OF JAPANESE HISTORY

The following is a short outline of the relevant periods of Japanese history, with a focus on military aspects.

During the Kamakura Period or *Kamakura-jidai* (1185–1333) armies consisted entirely of small groups of mounted samurai warriors and their followers on foot, who were mostly limited to supporting roles. The subsequent Muromachi Period (1336–1573) experienced the Onin War of 1467–1477, which especially devastated the Imperial and Shogunal capital now known as Kyoto. Following this, a large number of regional and local fiefdoms achieved virtual independence. Their leaders, the *daimyo*, were samurai and led samurai armies against internal and external opposition, ever keen on securing and expanding their territories. This permanent "civil war" was in reality a war between members of the same class, the samurai, but at the expense of other classes, especially the farming population. It escalated in the 16th century during a period also known as *Sengoku-jidai*, which roughly means a "country at war" – a term which was borrowed from Chinese ancient history. The military means employed by these daimyo to defeat their rivals are the focus of this book. There were three great leaders of samurai, all-time greats of Japanese history who made sure the number of competing fiefdoms got smaller and smaller until one family controlled all of Japan. These were Oda Nobunaga (d. 1582), Toyotomi Hideyoshi (d. 1598), and Tokugawa Ieyasu (d. 1616).

The Sengoku Period is usually considered to have begun with the Onin War in 1467. As for when it ended, there are several possible dates. In 1590, Toyotomi Hideyoshi overcame his last major domestic challenger, the Hojo family of Odawara, and soon embarked on an invasion of Korea with China in his sights. 1598 (death of Hideyoshi on his futon in his castle of Fushimi) is another option, but one might also look to 1603, when Tokugawa Ieyasu took the vacant supreme office of shogun for himself. His family kept it for more than 250 years. In 1614/15, the Tokugawa took on the remaining organized samurai opposition and destroyed the Toyotomi stronghold of Osaka Castle. The last major battle involving tens of thousands of samurai troops took place at Hara Castle on the Shimabara Peninsula in 1638. This era is the focus of this book. One might feel tempted to call it "The Long Sengoku Period" (analogous to stretching the "Long 19th Century" in Europe to 1914, when a war started that was to change everything). In Japan, all these events lead as important steps into the Edo Period (1603–1867) which saw the country under Tokugawa control. There were still events and trends relevant to military affairs, especially in the first and in the final decades of the Edo Period, but the nature of their work changed for the samurai class from fighting to training and administrating, and many became nostalgic for the past, when huge armies fought under famous banners and heroic deeds were done. This produced a large number of historical records that form much of the basis for studying Sengoku military history.

One striking feature of samurai armies in the Sengoku Period is, despite their deadly functionality, the great sense of aesthetics visible in everything from weapons, armour and clothing design to heraldry and ceremonies and related arts. While certainly not new in the 16th century, this trend peaked in the Azuchi-Momoyama Period (1568–1603), which also covers much of our period of interest. The double name refers to Oda Nobunaga´s revolutionary new castle of Azuchi on the shores of Lake Biwa, and to a famous peach tree-covered hill (Momoyama) close to Kyoto on which Toyotomi Hideyoshi built his castle of Fushimi, in which he died and which became the scene of a fierce siege in 1600 (castles and sieges are covered in-depth in volume 2). Azuchi-Momoyama is the culmination of ingenious design in fields as varied as military and residential architecture, painting, gardening, pottery, tea ceremony, clothing, and samurai-related items. The period is colourful yet subtle, striking but simple, and finds, arguably, its most amazing expression in samurai armour design.

Azuchi-Momoyama designers as well as weapons and armour manufacturers, and even contemporary Japanese culture at large were quick to understand which important technological and creative sparks were coming from the world outside of Japan. In 1542/43 the first *nambanjin* arrived, more or less incidentally, in Japan. The term describes the first Europeans arriving in advanced ships; first, the Portuguese, then Spaniards, Dutch and English. The *nambanjin* introduced modern firearms (arquebus and cannon) to Japan, and those daimyo who had the insight as well as the geographical situation and the financial means to quickly adopt the new technologies were among those who held a decisive advantage in the upcoming final rounds of the match for ultimate power in Japan. In turn, the impact of firearms dictated a strengthening of armour and changed the appearance of samurai armies on the battlefield.

Takeda Shingen (1521-1573)
Kofu, Takeda Shrine

Together with his arch-rival Uesugi Kenshin (1530-1578) Shingen is viewed as a model *daimyo* (territorial lord) of the Sengoku Period. Men like Shingen had to be constantly on guard while trying to enlarge their lands. This was only possible due to their highly sophisticated, professionally operated military machines. This book is about how men like Takeda Shingen achieved this.

Basics of Japanese Military History c. 1600

The image of a samurai as a knightly individual fighter with his sword as his main weapon only had some connection to reality when there were no more pitched battles to be fought in Japan, in the Edo Period after 1638 until right into the middle of the 19th century. Before the 15th/16th century the main armament of the samurai was the Japanese longbow, *yumi*, until supplanted by the *yari*, a lance of varying length to be used for both thrusting and cutting. At the same time both economic and political developments made possible the enlargement of the armies fielded, which reduced the opportunities for achieving individual glory. Battle was no longer about several hundred or a few thousand men opposing each other, but often several tens of thousands of combatants, even around 100,000 in one army. The samurai countered this trend by relying on their eye-catching individual heraldry to remain visible even among a large number of men, but as an individual fighters they mostly disappeared from organized warfare.

The basic tactical units of our period were organized formations on foot fighting with lances or pikes up to 6.3 metres long. Next to them there were mixed units of arquebus handgunners and longbowmen who tried to weaken enemy attacks. As opposed to contemporary Europe, Japanese tactics remained focused on the attack. Fighting was basically a running affair; those who stopped and stood still became prime targets, and shields carried by samurai were almost never used. Even during sieges heavily outnumbered defenders sometimes sallied out in search for a decisive encounter on open ground. With regard to this martial tradition, American troops in the Pacific War of 1941–1945 should not have been surprised by the behaviour of their Japanese opponents who often enough only seemed to know one technique to defend a position – a furious, sometimes suicidal charge on foot. Also in the decades around 1600, the contrast between Japanese and European military practises is likewise considerable. European armies relied on *Gewalthaufen*, *tercios* and *brigades* – massive, slow-moving formations with heavily armed infantry soldiers – whereas Japanese were more lightly armed and thus more agile, and generally drawn up no deeper than two ranks with some distance between the various elements of a unit. Overall, lighter armour enabling dynamic movement and easy use of weapons were deemed a better protection than heavy steel and cumbersome weapons which tired the soldier more quickly.

The explosion of samurai armies in numbers was only possible by increasingly including members of the farming class *(yakusho)* as foot soldiers *(ashigaru)*. This new type of fighting man initially was lacking in training and did not have the skills at arms reached by men born into samurai families who trained all their lives. However, in a group working together well they were capable even of overwhelming a mounted samurai. In the 15th century, ashigaru were part-time warriors who were called up from their fields when war broke out. Only toward the end of the 16th century and only when serving daimyo with considerable means did they manage to rise to the status of military professionals permanently removed from tilling the fields. Of course it was not possible to equip them as lavishly as the old elite of samurai who generally brought their own arms and armour. Sometimes ashigaru only wore a cone-shaped iron hat *(jingasa)*, which famously could also be used for cooking rice over a camp fire. Instead of complete sets of individually crafted armour ashigaru received, on loan, body armour from their lord which was mass-produced, basic and painted with his military badges, thus creating units that resembled uniformed troops.

In any case, it became more difficult to recognize individual fighters and units in the field. This trend was enhanced by the spread of *mempo*, armoured face masks for samurai. This development facilitated the introduction of ever larger numbers of heraldic banners, which could be several metres tall. Individual fighters started to wear small flags and other heraldic objects on the backs of their armour, which either indicated their unit or their individuality as samurai (*sashimono* – volume 2 covers the topic of heraldry extensively). With this system in place, complete uniformity of dress was not necessary for purposes other than representation.

As for firearms, these were used since the middle of the 16th century. Arquebus (*teppo* or *tanegashima*) availability grew quickly; cannon however, were usually limited to static warfare because they were too cumbersome for fast-moving Japanese battlefield tactics. Arquebus fire, especially when used in salvoes by a large number of soldiers, could break an attacking formation of mounted samurai (who rarely numbered more than 10% of an army in this period) and the foot soldiers following the horse. Firing teppo is a standard feature of historical festivals and reenactments in Japan today. The shooters often wear elaborate samurai armour – which contradicts historical reality where the members of arquebus units (*teppo-tai*) belonged to the ashigaru class and were valued only for their military contribution, not for their social status.

As it is so often the case in situations in which very similar armies oppose each other, it was hard to gain that decisive strategic advantage needed to win big. This mostly

Samurai in command with ashigaru foot soldiers in front of field fortifications
Re-enactment of the battle of Sekigahara 1600, 2000.

depended on the daimyo´s or lord´s ability to mobilize all of his territory´s resources and forge them into an effective fighting force which was superior in morale, numbers and material. Economic and diplomatic savvy, a long-term military strategy and, finally, careful manoeuvring on the battlefield could produce that slight advantage that would become the foundation of a great victory.

During battle the commander-in-chief was expected to sit, ostensibly unshaken by events occurring around him, on his camp stool in his headquarters at the rear of his army's centre. He or his staff officers were expected to direct their forces masterfully, not to fight themselves. After the battle came the time to receive reports about brave warriors who had proved their mettle by presenting the heads of defeated enemies for formal review. Rewards were to be handed out, even castles or entire provinces could be gained by top generals. All the while the leader's thoughts were supposed to centre on the next campaign because in the end there was only to be one winner – Tokugawa Ieyasu, who coined the famous aphorism "After a battle, tighten the cords of your helmet." When Ieyasu became shogun in 1603 he could look back on a long career which epitomized one virtue above all others: patience, coupled with the ability to grab each opportunity that presented itself. He brought power to his family and mostly peace to his country for centuries.

ARMS AND ARMOUR

Samurai

Most samurai fighting in the late 16th and early 17th centuries were armoured in a much simpler, cheaper, but still more effective manner than their ancestors in past centuries. This was especially the case for those fighting on foot.

The usually dome-shaped helmet *(kabuto)* was often reinforced with rivets. In the older style, helmet bowls were constructed from up to 62 plates which were held by up to 1700 rivets. However, in the Sengoku period many fighting men wore helmets welded together using only three (*hineno* style) or five (*zunari* style) large steel parts. The neck protector *(shikoro)* became smaller and even the two small folded-back metal plates protecting the sides *(fukigaeshi)* were much smaller now or even disappeared altogether. High-ranking samurai had heraldic or other spectacular devices mounted on the front *(maedate)* or at the back *(ushirodate)* of their helmet bowl. Some helmets in the *kawari kabuto* category ("strange helmets") could have large objects sculpted from strong paper hardened and sealed by lacquer on top of their bowl. Other helmet types showed European influence, especially when pear- or peach-shaped or in the form of the morion helmets then popular in Portugal and Spain. These "exotic" helmet bowls were integrated into Japanese elements of armour such as added neck protection and design ornaments.

Beneath their helmets, samurai often wore their long hair as it was or tied together. A headband typically made of white, blue or brown cloth absorbed sweat and supported the helmet. As a cheap alternative, this headband could be reinforced by armour elements at the front, with no helmet worn.

The classical *o-yoroi* box-like suit of armour had gone completely out of fashion for fighting purposes in the Sengoku Period. Another traditional type, the tighter-fitting, lighter *do-maru*, also lost ground during the 16th century but was still in evidence. The *do-maru* consists of many horizontal small armour plates held together by lacing cords. It allowed more freedom of movement than the heavy *o-yoroi*, but it did not offer good protection against firearms and was not cheap to manufacture. Among new forms of cuirasses, Western-influenced, duck-breasted (peascod) *namban-do* appeared. These consisted of massive steel pieces for the front and the back, offering superior protection. With their arms and legs more lightly armoured than in Europe, *namban-do* wearers were still agile. Recent research quoted by Trevor Absolon raises the thesis that real *namban-do* only arrived in 1600 in Japan when Tokugawa Ieyasu was able to lay his hands on what was inside the Dutch ship *De Liefde*, piloted by the Englishman John Adams. This included twelve or so such cuirasses, and it is possible that the *namban-do* suit worn by Ieyasu at Sekigahara the same year originally came from the hold of the Dutch ship. However, Japanese metalworkers were, just as with arquebus guns, highly capable to pick up the new techniques needed to produce "Made in Japan" *namban-do*.

Genuinely Japanese strong armour came in types such as *okegawa-do* and *yukinoshita-do*. Date Masamune (1567–1636), Lord of Sendai, equipped many or all of his troops with the latter type of cuirass, which also became known as *sendai-do*. Such armour was sometimes decorated as if it consisted of rows of armour plates laced together, but in reality it was made of only a few large, sturdy pieces tightly joined together, protecting front and back. A cuirass made this way gave its wearer a better chance to survive arquebus bullets fired from close range (30 metres or closer), although some simple armour pieces were only about 1 mm thick.

Another part of many suits of armour were face masks. *Mempo* covered chin, cheeks, and nose; *hanbo* only cheeks and chin; *happuri* cheeks and forehead, while *somen* covered the entire face except for the eyes. Often face masks showed terrifying designs produced to intimidate opponents, inspired in no small part by the heroic No theatre beloved by many samurai. The vulnerable part around the samurai´s throat was protected by a gorget, either a hanging piece of armour called *ayodarekake*, or by the more popular *nodawa*. In this arrangement there was a protective ring of iron around the neck with a suspended piece of armour in front.

Most forms of body armour consisted of two major parts *(ni-mai-do)* with a front and back half. Both pieces were joined on the left side by a hinge and fastened with cords on the right side, with the back part usually overlapping the front protection. Shoulders were protected by stiff stripes of armour, often hinged at the upper back side of the cuirass. As with older models of armour, the abdomen of the wearer was protected by a number of armour plates suspended from the bottom of the cuirass. The number of these *kusazuri* could vary between four and many more, although seven was widespread during the Sengoku period. Horsemen wore additional thigh protection plates called haidate under their *kusazuri*, suspended from the hip and reaching down to above the knees. Lower legs and arms usually were also protected, with greaves being called *sune-at*e and arm protectors *kote*. Both leg and arm protection had a tendency peculiar to the Sengoku Period of increasingly consisting of chainmail, strengthened by small steel plates. Greaves were not worn by all fighting men; some only had sturdy gaiters made of cloth tied around their lower legs. Shoulder plates *(sode)*, which had been huge and cumbersome with *o-yoroi* sets, became smaller and smaller and could even disappear by dissolving into the new armour pattern of the *kote*.

Actor dressed up as Oda Nobunaga (1534–1582)
Ise Sengoku-Mura (theme park)

Oda Nobunaga was the son of a minor daimyo in Owari Province. After many years of fighting Nobunaga rose to become the dominant military power-broker in central Japan. His appearance is typical for Sengoku Period lords. He wears a valuable suit of armour made of many metal plates lavishly laced together with blue and red silk cords. As Nobunaga also sports a *jimbaori* surcoat made of silk and heavy wool he wears reduced armour on his neck, shoulders and arms. However, lower arms, thighs, and legs from knee to ankle are well protected. All textiles are high quality, with precious metal threads woven into gorgeous patterns (see volume 2 for more on the clothes of the samurai). Instead of a helmet Nobunaga wears a more comfortable *eboshi* court cap with unhardened fibres so that it does not stand upright. This style of eboshi can serve as a useful padding for a helmet which was, when not actually worn, always carried close to the lord by several retainers along with his weapons. As for footwear, even wealthy Sengoku samurai stopped wearing fur shoes, instead preferring *tabi* socks and simple straw sandals (*zori*) like all other troops did.

Samurai kneeling with long pikes, supported by ashigaru. On the battlefield, samurai *yari* troops were often placed behind a screen of long *yari* ashigaru.

Their back flags *(sashimono)* show a coat of arms called *maru mitsuhiki* which was used by the Kikkawa, one of the branches of the powerful Mori clan of Western Japan (photo from the Sekigahara Reenactment, 2000).

Helmets from Sengoku to Edo Periods in various Japanese Museum Collections

Ribbed helmet bowls (*suji-kabuto*, **Fig. 4 & 5**) appeared in the 16th century. Fig. 5 is a classic example of a helmet made for fighting, not parade. Its bowl is made of twelve parts and lacquered in black. The heavy *shikoro* neck protector is laced in blue. This helmet was lost by a Takeda samurai on the battlefield of Nagashino in 1575. Some helmets were decorated by small or large ornaments including spectacular designs such as the crab pincers of **Fig. 4**. However, it was more common for helmets to have a mechanism in front (as in **Fig. 1, 2, 4 & 5**) to fix *maedate* ornaments such as the flat holed disk of **Fig. 4**. **Fig. 1 & 2** show some European influences, especially the *namban*-style bowl of **Fig. 2** could be an import piece augmented by Japanese elements. **Fig. 1** belongs to the genre of *kawari kabuto* (literally "strange" or unusual helmets). It is modeled on a towel slung around the head (*oki tenugui-nari kabuto*). However, the most widespread mass-producible helmet type of the Sengoku Period was the *zunari kabuto* **Fig. 3**, welded together from three or (here) five pieces of steel. Samurai and ashigaru were administered in different units. However, in battle samurai sometimes formed one line backing up a line of pike-armed ashigaru, or ashigaru with shorter *yari* stood behind samurai.

Headwear and Hair Styles

Between the 8th and 16th centuries the *eboshi* (sometimes referred to as "court cap") was the most widespread piece of male headwear. Receiving one's own *eboshi* marked the transition between boyhood and adulthood as celebrated especially in samurai families as a part of the male coming-of-age ceremony, *genpuku*. This custom had originated within the imperial family, spread to the Ashikaga shogunal family and the warrior class, and was even adopted by commoners. By the 16th c. some inhabitants of towns and even some better-situated peasants wore *eboshi*.

The basic model of eboshi was the *tate* or "standing" *eboshi*, **Fig. 12**. Lacquer was applied to harden the black gauze material, resulting in a stiff cap. In the Sengoku Period this old style was mainly limited to very formal wear fit for the Imperial Court in Kyoto or certain events involving leading daimyo. Samurai adopted a style for which the eboshi was folded several times and secured by a cord, leaving room for the hair knot (*ori eboshi*, **Fig. 9 & 10**). Obviously, this style of wearing an eboshi provided a good rest for a helmet and it could be worn with or without such heavy headwear. **Fig. 11** shows the first step of folding an eboshi. The silk cord used to secure

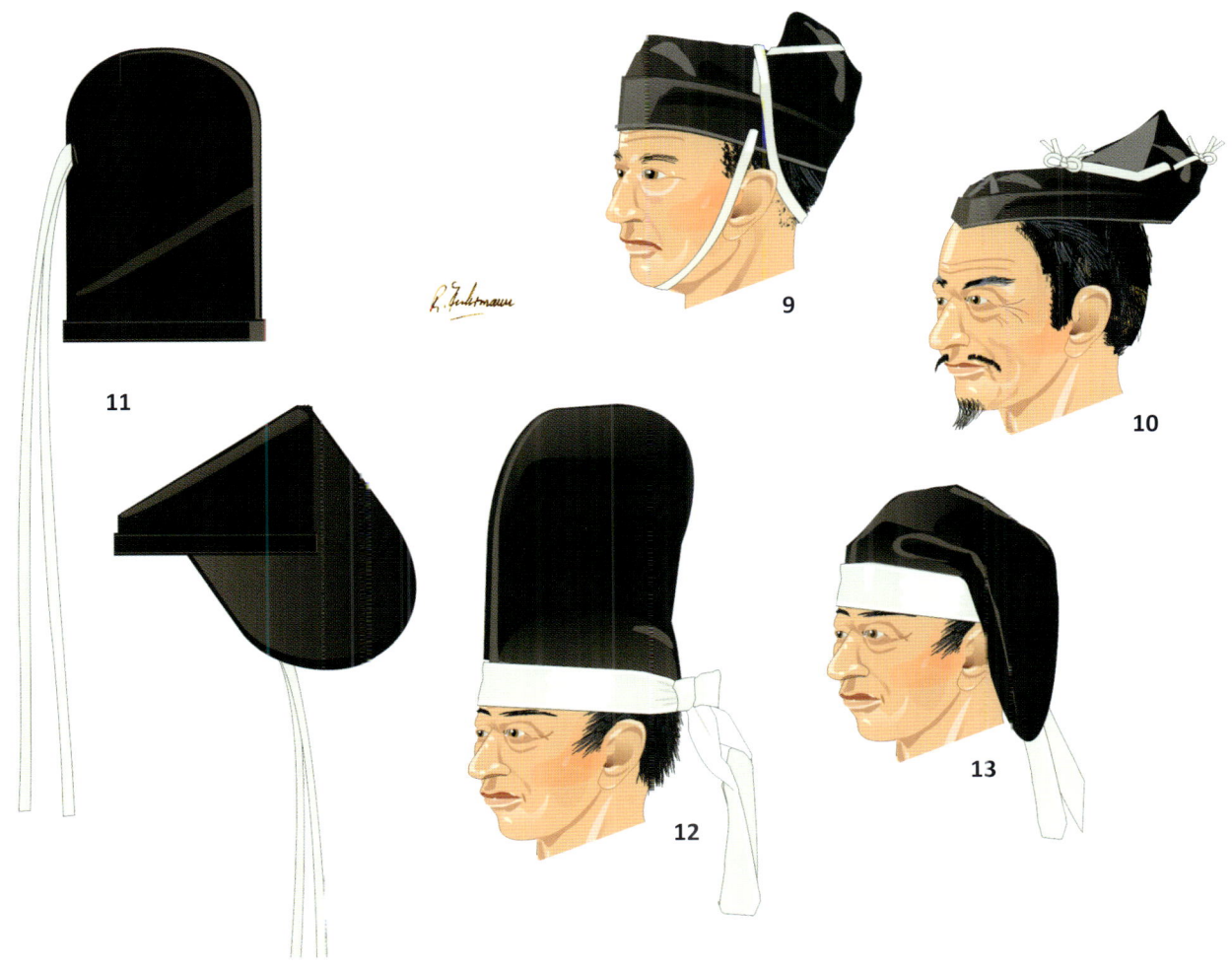

the cap, called *eboshi gake*, was not always white; certain ceremonies required a differently coloured *eboshi gake* to be worn. The *motodori* (hair knot) was also considered a sign of high rank and srequired careful grooming. It was helpful in fixing a folded *ori eboshi* to the head. However, as the 16th c. progressed, more men decided to go bareheaded or simply slung a towel around their forehead. For fighting men, this could be reinforced by sewing steel armour plates to it (**Fig. 8**).

Samurai had usually worn their full hair long or tied it up in knots or tufts (**Fig. 1, 2, 4, 6**). In the 16th c. the custom of shaving the forehead clean started to spread among samurai (**Fig. 3, 5, 8**) until in the 17th c. almost all well-groomed men sported their hair in this style. Boys who had not yet had their genpuku ceremony shaved their heads but left part of their hair growing just above their forehead (**Fig. 7**). Long hair could be tied up in neat, brush-like tufts like in **Fig. 5**, which is based on Toyotomi Hideyoshi's appearance. **Fig. 2** is a classical style of wearing a helmet on long, open hair, which could be seen under the *shikoro* neck guard or come out of the small hole found at the tops of some helmet bowls. As for facial hair, a wide array of styles was worn, ranging from Chinese sage-style to fiercely flowing full beards. In the Sengoku Period many samurai wore moustaches. However, in the Edo Period more and more men preferred to be clean-shaven, as a sizeable beard came to be looked upon as something uncivilized.

Body Armour

Top:

Haramaki ("belly-wrapping") armour
National Museum, Tokyo
This suit is made up of body protection and five armour plates suspended from the hip (*kusazuri*). It has a "coward's piece" at its back which covers the typical gap between the five regular elements of armour. Since a samurai was not expected to turn his back on the enemy (and flee) this part of some people's armour received the appropriately unpleasant nickname. The two rings at the back indicate that large *sode* (shoulder armour) could be tied on. *Haramaki* armour was standard in the early Sengoku Period and could still be seen later being worn by foot soldiers and samurai unable to afford more modern equipment, or by those with a strong nostalgic trait.

Left:

Armour Detail, *National Museum Tokyo*
This shoulder detail belongs to a more modern, Western-influenced suit of armour, which is an extreme opposite of haramaki armour. There are only two large steel plates forming a cuirass, and shoulder armour (sode) has almost vanished. All that remains are three small rows sitting on top of armoured sleeves made of small steel plates, chain mail, leather, and textile fabrics.

Suit of Armour (Type *Iozane-odoshi nimaido gusoku*)
Shimabara Castle Museum, Nagasaki Prefecture

The cuirass has a breast and a back plate (*nimai-do*), both of which are made up of small metal scales (*iozane*) laced together with black and white cords. The helmet is *suji-kabuto* type, decorated with a golden *maedate* in the shape of a fan. This suit of armour comes with its stowage and transportation chest which is painted with a family crest, consisting of three bars, perhaps representing the kanji character "three", surrounded by melon flower details (*kuwa no uchi ni mitsubiki*). The armour exemplifies late Sengoku (Azuchi-Momoyama) Era tastes also in its colourful appearance, which became more subdued later during the Edo period. One origin of having differently coloured parts in one suit of armour is the old samurai habit of exchanging helmets with a friend or relative before battle so that they would stand out to each other, support each other, and to bear witness to each other's exploits when it came to claiming rewards after battle. Also, suits of armour owned by less affluent combatants did not always come from one source but could be ensembles composed of pieces made to order, found in an arsenal, loaned by relatives, bought in markets, or taken from battlefields.

In addition to this, Momoyama tastes were flamboyant, with bold colours and colour combinations that can look stunning even to this day. Although apparently made to order, the suit shown above is not rare in combining metal armour components lacquered in bright red, brownish red and black. Natural steel colour, rusted steel, blue, white, silver, or golden lacquer could also be seen on suits of armour as well as multi-coloured cords and precious metal ornaments.

Photographs from the Sekigahara Re-Enactment in 2000

At the other end of armour quality compared to the suits shown on preceding pages came armour given on loan to ashigaru foot soldiers. These examples show *tatami-do* style armour which consisted of small rectangular metal plates sewn onto textiles. The rectangular shape of the plate reminded Japanese of tatami mats used for many purposes in daily as well as in military life. Note multiple ways of attaching cloth and leather bags, bundles and bamboo drinking flasks to the belt or carrying them over the shoulder or around the hip

Ashigaru armour belonging to the Hojo family

Since the Hojo collapsed in 1590, this piece from the Sengoku Period is very rare. The *do* (cuirass) consists of a solid breastplate with the Hojo crest lacquered on in gold and several rows of lamellae tied with blue lace at the bottom. (Chiba Castle Museum)

The dwindling size of shoulder protection left the neck vulnerable. A new piece of armour was needed and came in the shape of an armoured yet padded collar which could reach out to cover most of the shoulders. These *tate-eri* often consisted of small hexagonal armour plates sewn onto ray skin, and heavy cloth bound in leather *(kikko)*. Whatever remained unarmoured at the joint between shoulders and upper arms could be covered by small plates named *kohire* (= "little wings").

There was one vulnerable part of the torso which could not be perfectly covered without losing too much freedom of movement: the armpits remained a target for *yari* (lances), especially when wielded by foot soldiers against cavalry. The knee pits were also difficult to protect effectively.

Most armour was lacquered. This happened not just for display but also as a protection against rust. Black dominated as the main colour, but red and brown hues were not rare either. Extravagant lords sometimes wore their armour lacquered in gold or silver and did the same with armour parts worn by their elite troops. Another method of protecting armour surfaces was to have them systematically and evenly rust which gave the suit a rough surface with a distinct colour. The Japanese climate with its high humidity and intensive rainy season was rough especially on the laces binding individual elements of armour together. These were made of silk, other textiles or leather, and needed frequent repair and replacement.

In our era it became popular for samurai, especially those equipped for foot combat, to wear their long sword *(katana)* and short sword *(wakizashi)* in corresponding design and similar scabbards, thus creating the famous matching pairs sought after by today´s collectors. These pairs were worn thrust into the *obi* (cloth belt) of the samurai, in order to be drawn easily at a moment´s notice. Horsemen usually opted for one shorter sword or a dagger, plus a longer, straight-bladed sword mounted in the older *tachi* style, meaning it was hung horizontally from the left hip, edge downward. The blade tended to be shorter than in the preceding century so the *tachi* could also be used for melee fighting on foot. In fact, many old swords with good blades were shortened in the Sengoku Period, which means that valuable inscriptions containing information about swordsmiths are now lost to us. The upper part of the *tachi* scabbard as well as sword hilts were often wrapped in silk cords to protect them from wear and tear and to allow a firm grip. In any case, the samurai´s main armament was now, in any case, the *yari* (lance), and swords were usually drawn only towards the end of a battle, if at all. This is also evident from the fact that among a samurai´s personal retainers the *omochi-yari kasugi* or *yarimochi* who carried his master´s lance was the best paid, at least in the 17th century (*Zohyo Monogatari*, p. 19). There were many types of yari, varying in length of blade and shaft, and also in the shape of the blade. Tsukahara Bokuden (1489–1571) advised young samurai not to select a lance whose handling overtaxed their own strength; Bokuden surely was an expert whose handbook "The Hundred Rules of War", penned shortly before his death, was read by many samurai. It contains advice on many topics dear to a Sengoku Period samurai, and was written by a famous samurai who had been in 37 battles and won countless one-on-one fights.

While the sword was important to a samurai both in practical and in psychological ways, the bow, a former main armament, was now relegated to specialized archer units, and equally obsolete was the *naginata*, a kind of sword lance, which mainly became the self-defence weapon of choice for samurai women.

Samurai were motivated by loyalty to their lords, but also by the desire to become famous and receive individual rewards and promotions. It was established practice to recognize feats such as *ichiban-nori* (the samurai who was first into a castle or on its walls), *ichiban-* and *niban-yari* (first and second kill with a yari), or *kuzushigiwa* (someone who broke up an enemy formation with a kill). Heads were taken off slain enemies, presented to superiors and carefully registered. A small group of senior samurai, the *metsuke*, were responsible for doing the groundwork for fair rewards to everybody who qualified. However ferocious a samurai charge might be, the actual risk of losing one´s life was perhaps not that grave, as the handbook *Zohyo Monogatari* has a lowly *umatori* (a servant tending to horses) comment: "Samurai often talk about being killed as a result of their feats in war… (but) there is not such a great chance of being killed – if I am honest, that is." (p. 32). Samurai armour protected a man rather well, and perhaps their less armoured or unarmoured retainers faced a bigger risk.

Haramaki Armour Bound in Leather
National Museum Tokyo

This suit of repaired armour is a very rare survivor. Most samurai in the Sengoku Period would have been astonished to hear that it was owned and proudly displayed by a national museum. The basic *haramaki* pattern is the same as for the example on p. 20 (without the "coward's piece" – note the typical gap in the protection of the back), but the armour's surface is almost completely covered in leather. In the Muromachi and Sengoku Periods broken or otherwise damaged armour would often be repaired as much as possible and then bound in leather to hold it together and to hide its weaknesses. It was used by low-ranking warriors or retainers who did not have access to new armour. See also Fig. 4 on p. 31 for a reconstruction of a foot soldier wearing this type of armour.

Conical Helmet (*jingasa*)
Former Residence of the Inaba, Daimyo at Usuki (Oita Prefecture)

The front of these Edo Period jingasa is painted with the Inaba clan's main crest, *sumikirigaku ni mitsu no ji* (the numeral "3" inside a truncated square). The backs curiously are painted with different family crests, indicating that these jingasa may actually have been made for samurai who were allowed to add their own family crest, not ashigaru. In these peaceful times, lighter styles of armour and helmets were preferred for comfort, and samurai took to wearing jingasa on various occasions.

Ashigaru Armour and Jingasa Conical Helmets

The types of body armour shown are *hotoke-do* as for **Fig. 1**, and *okegawa-do* as for **Fig. 2**. A = front view, b = rear view. Such armour made of iron, lacquer, leather, and cords including *kusazuri* hip protection and helmet usually weighed about 5 kg. The suits were administered by the lord's arsenal staff and typically painted with his family crest or any other design he saw suitable (*ai-jirushi*, or badges).
1a–b Ogasawara Clan. The design motive is the kanji character "o", the first from the family name Ogasawara.
2a–b Mori Clan. Front: two folded fans (*daikichi ogi*), an auspicious motive. Back: Stylized depiction of sweets on rice (*hishi mochi*). Adding a design to the back plate is as unusual as it is to use two different designs on one single suit of arsenal armour.
3 Toda Clan. Lacquered bright red, the six-star motive is repeated on each of the hip plates.
4 Three gold bars, possibly marking a specific unit in the army of an unknown clan.
5 Itakura Clan. This is one of two formal *kamon* (crests) of this family. Itakura Shigemasa (1588–1638) was killed in the Shimabara War against Christian rebels, the last large-scale samurai battle for over 200 years.
6 The Tokugawa Family's Owari Line. As there were so many lords related to the shogun it would not have been helpful if all of them had used the famous Tokugawa hollyhock crest (*aoi no mon*) on their troops' armour. The *ai-jirushi* chosen here consists of two mountains. The visor added to the conical helmet is unusual.
7 Sanada Clan, sporting one of several known variants of a ladder, with the associated message "Luck is on the rise".
8 Ishida Mitsunari, hapless leader of the Western army at Sekigahara in 1600, where this piece was most likely actually worn. It is lacquered in a reddish-brown hue and decorated with Mitsunari's motto *Dai ichi, dai man, dai kichi* ("Great victory, long life, much happiness", cf. frontispiece).
9 Sakakibara Clan, made of rusted iron and leather. The wheel motive (*kuruma no mon*) is the family's main crest. The Sakakibara also issued suits of armour lacquered red with the same mon in black.
10 Matsudaira Nobotsuna (1596–1662), relative of the shogun and victorious general at Shimabara.
11 Sengoku Clan, using the kanji character "mu" meaning "nothing" or more specifically "This world means nothing", expressing a samurai's readiness to leave it at any time, dying a glorious death (see Kakizaki in vol. 2, pp. 76-77 & 79).

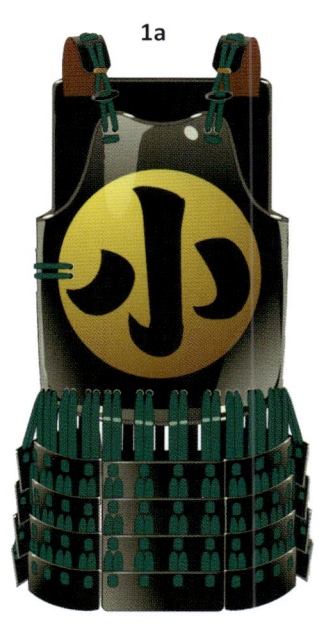

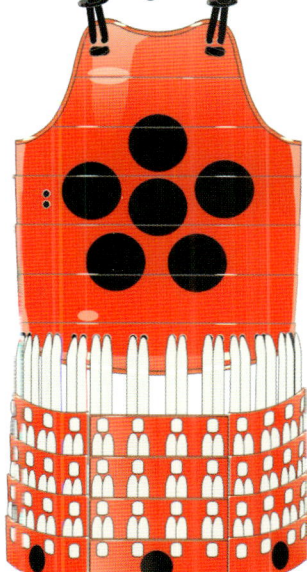

Ashigaru Armour and Jingasa Conical Helmets

12 Ashigaru helmet belonging to the foot life guards of Date Masamune (1567–1636). A spectacular piece using a massively exaggerated jingasa shape to top a higher-grade samurai helmet, called *jingasa-nari kabuto.*

13a–b Sengoku Clan. High quality black-lacquered body armour with gold lacquer applied to the jingasa, indicating that this ensemble might have been used by elite troops. Besides the kamon of **Fig. 11** the Sengoku also used the crest of an old Chinese coin on armour and banners. It originally belonged to Oda Nobunaga and was given as a token of appreciation to four samurai/daimyo families: Sengoku, Mizuno, Yamauchi, and Kuroda.

14, 15 Unidentified Clan, perhaps Hori?

16 Suekawa Clan.

17 Most likely Shimazu Clan, daimyo of Satsuma (Kagoshima). This is not a Christian motive but can be seen as a stylized horse snaffle or the kanji character "ju" for "10" in a circle.

18 Beautiful jingasa made of twelve metal strips. The crest is *kikyo-no-mon* (Chinese bellflower), belonging to the ancient Toki clan of Mino, later used by several families such as the Asano and the Akechi, claiming them as ancestors.

19 Snake's Eye motive (*hebi no me*), famously used by Kato Kiyomasa (1562–1611). This actual helmet was most likely made in the 18th c., when it became fashionable to flatten jingasa tops. Owned by the Kato of Ozu in today's Ehime Prefecture.

20 Jingasa from the battlefield museum at Nagashino in Shizuoka Prefecture. Jingasa helmets consisted of three basic elements: the actual conical helmet, a padded cushion underneath (*zabuton*), and cotton or leather straps to fix the helmet under the chin (*ago-himo,* not shown here). There are surviving helmets made of many different materials: iron/steel, leather, bamboo, wicker, hardened paper and lacquer.

21 In the field, many ashigaru added **a neck flap made of sturdy cotton cloth or bast or hemp fibres** to their jingasa. Often this was simply left in natural undyed colours, but could be dyed in any colour or sport patterns stencilled in.

Ashigaru

The increase in army sizes that started in the 15th century offered an opportunity to many an able-bodied young fellow to leave the hard life of the peasant and try to climb the social ladder by entering into military service with a lord. The most famous example of such a careerist is Toyotomi Hideyoshi, who was born in 1537 to peasant parents and ended his life in 1598 as the undisputed ruler of all Japan. He served Oda Nobunaga as an ashigaru in his young years. Nobunaga, himself a highly unconventional daimyo, noticed the young lad's intelligence and resourcefulness. The various stages of Hideyoshi's unfolding career are well-described in Yoshikawa Eiji's epic historical novel "Taiko" (published and reprinted in English as "Taiko: An Epic Novel of War and Glory in Feudal Japan"). Other famous self-made leaders of samurai include Hideyoshi's man Hachizuka Masakatsu (1525–1585), who started his career leading a gang of robbers and ended it as a rich daimyo lording over his own fief in Shikoku, and Oda Nobunaga's early rival Saito Dosan (1494–1556), also known as the Viper of Mino, who began his career as an oil seller.

Ashigaru literally means light or fast feet. These foot soldiers traditionally went either unarmoured or sported just basic protection offered by *hara-ate* type body armour. This only protected the front of the torso with tiny plates suspended from the hip, also only in front. The back was frequently unprotected, and so were arms, legs and the head, which was often covered by a soft *eboshi* cap worn by adult men during most of the Sengoku Period. A part-armoured headband and cheek-protectors usually were the best head protection available to such men. *Hara-ate* were made of small rows or lamellae of armour plate tied together. This basic set could be augmented by items found on a battlefield or among obsolete pieces in the lord's armoury.

The Sengoku Period however saw the introduction of a type of armour and even helmets that were easier to produce: *tatami-do*, named after the rectangular woven mats covering the floor in a Japanese house. For *tatami-do*, small rectangular pieces of armour were sewn onto thick textiles (cloth or leather). This could be strengthened by using elements of chain mail. Besides their inexpensiveness, *tatami-do* were also easy to fold, store and transport, which attracted even some samurai to this style, albeit in more elaborate and better-made versions. However, as Trevor Absolon pointed out in 2017, pictorial evidence of *tatami-do* before c. 1600 is rare and most preserved suits of ashigaru armour are *okegawa-do*. So there remains a question mark concerning how far *tatami-do* armour had spread by the end of the Sengoku Period.

With increasing territories and financial capabilities, leading lords became able to order better and more complex suits of armour for their units of foot soldiers. The massive *okegawa-do* cuirass was easy to produce and could be augmented by shoulder protection as well as leg and arm armour. *Okegawa-do* belong to the new class of *tosei gusoku*, simply meaning "modern armour" that developed under European influence. *Tosei gusoku* in its various forms was cheaper and faster to mass-produce than older styles of armour. Further simplification meant that front and back armour plates could be hammered out from single sheets of steel. Some of these plates had a smooth surface *(hotoke-do)*, others were corrugated to simulate more classical armour. Of course, ashigaru armour quality was lower than that of the equipment worn by samurai; however, ashigaru were now uniformly clad in some form of armour, and their sense of unit-wide cohesion must have been growing.

When not in use, ashigaru suits of armour were kept in the lord's armoury under the supervision of an officer titled *gusoku bugyo* ("commissioner for armour"). Some pieces survive in multiple numbers complete with serial numbers at the inside (actually, kanji characters lacquered on). These arsenal armours were called *okashi gusoku* ("borrowed armour"). Despite an increasing degree of uniformity most units were not fitted out with uniforms of identical cloth but had back flags *(sashimono)* indicating for whom they fought and sometimes to which unit of the army they belonged.

Most Sengoku Period ashigaru were armed with one sword and a specialized weapon (lance, bow, or arquebus). The sword was their secondary armament, usually cheaply manufactured and neither too long nor too curvy for ease of drawing in close combat. Typically, ashigaru first put on their waist sash *(obi)*, then stuck the sword with its scabbard into it, and wore their armour on top, thus keeping the sword mounting stable. According to the handbook *Zohyo Monogatari*, it was recommended that ashigaru and *chugen* (auxilliaries) should wear a white cloth waist sash of about six feet length, which could also be used to carry wounded comrades on their backs.

However, the real trademark item most ashigaru around the year 1600 would be outfitted with was the conical helmet known as *jingasa*. This could be made of iron or leather, and the depth of the conical shape varied. *Jingasa* were lacquered in colours often matching the armour worn with them, and painted with the lord's emblems just as the body armour was.

Besides a large number of preserved items worn by ashigaru from the Edo Period and a smaller number from the Sengoku period, we have the illustrated ashigaru handbook of *Zohyo Monogatari* from 1657 as a prime source. The pictures show well-equipped ashigaru wearing borrowed armour and *jingasa* which are painted with their lord's marks or badges, often in matching suits. These badges were called *ai-jirushi* and could be based on the daimyo's coats of arms *(kamon)*, but more often they were other symbols.

Yamamoto Kansuke, 1501–1561, shown as one of Takeda Shingen´s famous Twenty-Four Generals

Kansuke was a *ronin* before he entered Takeda service in 1543. He rose to become *ashigaru-daisho* and then chief of staff *(gun-bugyo)*. Even though he was blind in one eye, lame and most likely very small even for his age, he was respected as a fierce warrior. On the battlefield of Kawanakajima in 1561 he threw himself at the charging enemy to buy time for his lord to regroup and to take responsibility for giving tactical advice that proved almost fatal for the Takeda. Yamamoto Kansuke did not survive this battle, but he left us some highly interesting writings as a great samurai legend.

Different Ashigaru Troop Types

1 ko-gashira (corporal) in golden five-part *yukinoshita-do* type armour. His appearance follows the *Zohyo Monogatari* handbook which shows some very elaborately outfitted ashigaru types. The corporal´s stick *ma-shaku* consists of a metal rod embedded in bamboo. More than a symbol of authority, it was a multi-purpose tool used for measuring shooting distances and providing a spare ramrod when needed. During battle, a ko-gashira in charge of arquebusiers would carry spare burning cotton fuses, often coiled around his left arm to help his men. Short ends of fuse could also be slung over small metal stands (*hinawa-kake*) which were stuck into the ground.

2 Teppo ashigaru (arquebusier) wearing full armour and kit including a bundle of spare ramrods on his back. He carries his cotton neck cloth wrapped around his head under the jingasa.

3 Yumi ashigaru (longbowman). Battered armour and torn clothing convey an image of how many foot soldiers might have looked like at the end of a campaign. The bamboo tube for storing water or other drink was called a *take-zutsu*.

4 Yari ashigaru (foot soldier with lance), Muromachi Period 14th–16th c. An iron forehead and cheek protector is added to his folded *eboshi* cap. His body armour is a leather-bound *haramaki* (see p. 25), while his clothing is the same that would have been worn by working men and peasants at the time. Around 1600 this man would have looked old-fashioned, but unlike **Fig. 1–3** many troops serving lesser lords did not yet have full modern equipment.

5 Generic ashigaru serving as a retainer with the baggage train or in another support role. His *tatami-do* armour consists of small metal plates and chain mail sewn to a thick leather or cloth garment. His helmet belongs to the wide-spread *zunari kabuto* type with simplified neck protection, but lacking a visor. The man wears spare straw sandals at his hip. These had a tendency not to last very long on marches and needed to be repaired or replaced often.

6–7 Storage boxes (*doran / tama-bako*) for arquebus supplies (cartridges, balls, powder etc.).

8 Large arrow quiver (*ya-bako*) for 50 or 100 arrows. Each missile unit included supply porters who carried containers such as this. In addition, each handgunner or bowman carried some supplies in pouches, sacks or quivers attached to his own body, and the ko-gashira had more supplies. These were the first to be used up, after that the men turned to their personal stocks while the ko-gashira replenished his supplies from the porters. This helps to explain the high ratio of NCOs and officers to rankers in missile units (often 1:5).

9 Wicker box used to transport stocks of rice.

10 Straw mat (*goza*) used for sitting or sleeping on when in camp. See **Fig. 3** for the method of carrying the mat. Fresh goza had a greenish colour which soon turned yellow-brown

11 Rations of pre-cooked rice wrapped in cloth (*hyoro-bukuro*).

12 Sack for a variety of items including arquebus balls.

13 Spare sandals (*zori*).

This *yumi-ashigaru* wears a solid one-piece black-lacquered breast plate with the red *kanji* character "hachi" (eight). In typical Sengoku fashion, the armour plates suspended from his hips are lacquered in a different colour, rusty red, and tied with indigo blue cords. His clothes are from various materials such as hemp, with cotton becoming available in large quantities towards the end of our period. Natural dyes applied to such textiles yielded colours of only modest intensity; however, they were often patterned (see vol.2 for details on cloth and patterns).

Warrior armed with a short lance
Besides his *yari*, the man has an inexpensive sword thrust into his *obi*. The sword not being too long or too curvy meant that it could be more easily drawn when it came to the secondary armament's use. Arms and legs are not well protected, and instead of a helmet he wears an iron forehead-and-cheek-mask (*happuri*). Short *hakama* trousers and short kimono sleeves indicate a hot period of the year. The textile leg protectors shown here are called *kyahan*.

Lightly-armoured ashigaru in *tatami-do* armour, proudly carrying an enemy head to present at after-battle inspections.

These marks were important to tell friend from foe and also provided a shared identity to men in the same army or unit. The motifs had to be clearly recognizable even for humble ashigaru who had no part in the pride of pedigree and heraldic trappings common to samurai houses. The same comment applies to battle flags and banners.

A number of surviving *jingasa* and suits of ashigaru armour are illustrated on pp. 27–28. Fig. 19 is one of six surviving *jingasa* painted with the famous snake eye motif. They were made in the late 18th c. for the fief of Ozu in today's Ehime Prefecture in Shikoku. Motif and geographic attribution indicate the daimyo family Kato as their original owners. Another snake eye is painted on the back of the *jingasa* and would most likely also have been on the matching suits of armour. The snake eye was actually a *kamon* (family crest) and was made famous by the Sengoku Period general Kato Kiyomasa (1562–1611). More often than actual family crests, *ai-jirushi* badges (badges or markings chosen by a lord) were used. Well-known *ai-jirushi* include the ladder used by the Sanada clan who rose to fame through their spirited defense of their castle of Ueno in 1600 during the Sekigahara campaign, and again in the battles for Osaka 1614/15. Such marks had to be eye-catching and simple, so we find discs, balls, triangles, mountain shapes or simple bars. Several bars could also be read as kanji characters for one, two, or three, useful for indicating different units within a daimyo's army. Hiragana characters were also useful for numbering. Some clans also decided to use a combination of one of their mon (coat of arms or crest) with a freely chosen motif such as stripes or bars (p. 28, fig. 18). Besides Tokugawa records of unit identification systems, there is very little information from the Sengoku Period on how which units were precisely marked.

Up to the 16th century all grown men wore their heads covered in public, usually with a cap made of black fabric, called an *eboshi*. This cap was also useful to soften the weight of a samurai helmet on the skull. However, increasingly it became acceptable to show one's uncovered, often partly shaved head in public. Among soldiers it became important to have some headdress made of cloth to support the helmet of their choice. The *jingasa* usually had an inner cushion called a *zabuton* to support it. The *jingasa* actually also incorporated some European influence since welding together large plates of iron had not been common before the arrival of the *nambanjin*.

Ashigaru usually had to carry their necessities when on campaign. This often included several days' rations of rice pressed into balls which were folded in a long piece of cloth and carried over the shoulders. This way of carrying supplies made quick meals possible in case the rice was pre-cooked, but it interfered with operating a bow, which is why ashigaru archers *(yumi-tai)* typically tied their rice balls to the backs of their armour. One rice ball was enough for one meal, and eating time came twice a day. Supply officers avoided handing out more than three days' worth of rice because they knew too well that excess rice with added yeast and water could be easily used to brew a crude form of sake!

Rural ashigaru accompanying their samurai master during a charge. (Scene from NHK television, 2014)

COMPOSITION AND COMMAND STRUCTURE OF A SAMURAI ARMY

Lord, Family, and Vassals

Each daimyo family had its own methods to organize their domain. However, there were some typical approaches characterizing contemporary military organization.

The band of family members and vassals was usually called a *kashindan*, headed by the governing lord who had to be addressed as "tono-sama" or "ue-sama". In the social hierarchy the lord was followed by his blood relatives *(shinrui)* who formed the *ichimon* ("first") group of vassals together with the *fudai*, a small number of long-serving, hereditary senior retainers who were, however, not related to the ruling family. Successful daimyo understood and utilized the different talents of their sons, brothers, and uncles. They found appropriate tasks for them and enabled them to play a useful role by granting them sufficient incomes and troop numbers, thus avoiding the domestic unrest which caused the downfall of not a few daimyo houses.

Lesser samurai in direct service to the daimyo often held rank as *hatamoto* (literally "men standing under a banner") and commanded individual small units or served in elite units of mounted samurai. One example is Okamoto Masahide, who served the Hojo of Odawara (see p. 41, 45 and case study on p. 47). Hatamoto were the backbone of a daimyo's military organization.

Members of the *ichimon* had vassals of their own *(kerai* or *kashin)* and raised their own banner/battle standard. Their military jobs could comprise command of a field unit or a wing of the army, or even serving as stand-in commander of an entire field army; *ichimon* members also were in charge of important castles and fortresses other than the lord's own main castle. Regular participation in the lord's council in peace and wartime was an indication of the top status of a vassal; his rank within the leading group was indicated by its seating order. Apart from the famous Takeda Shingen several other daimyo had groups of 20, 24, 28 or more or less top vassals/commanders/advisers associated with them over a period of time, some of them relatives, some not.

Samurai from this elite group not only commanded military units and castles, but also held other top administrative positions within the lord's territory. Besides the daimyo's son and heir, the most influential individuals were often the *karo*, a very small number of top retainers who served as house elders, senior advisers, "ministers", trusted military leaders and commanders of key networks of castles. The title *karo* as such was not exclusively a military title, but samurai administration meant that all top positions including civilian ones were held by samurai who also were members of their lord's military.

Samurai other than *ichimon* members did not sit on the lord's council. These were *kuni-shu* (landed gentry, usually organized in groups by district or province) and samurai from territories that had been added later or allies who fielded their own units. The Toyotomi labelled this group *shinzan-shu* ("new people"); the Tokugawa called them *tozama* ("outer allies", a term that would stick until the 19th century on the national level and mean eternal discrimination compared to the position of their old vassals, the *fudai* daimyo).

Command Structure

The leading vassals (*ichimon* and *karo*) held military titles and functions. In European Medieval parlance one might call many of them "bannerets" because they were allowed to fight under their own battle standard *(uma-jirushi)* as opposed to those who directly fought under the daimyo's own or his leading men's banners. They commanded independent and often self-contained units on campaign, much like a medieval banner or a later battalion/regiment. They typically lived in a major castle within the territory, which also was the base for their troops. As castle commanders (*jochu* or *jodai*) their manifold responsibilities included the maintenance of the military organization of the surrounding district and the defense of the lord's lands, which included keeping the castle and outposts well-guarded and repaired.

Other leading vassals served as *samurai-daisho*, commanding field units of several hundred or even a few thousand samurai and supporting troops. Above them there could be the position of *sodaisho*, a regular general commanding an entire army in case the lord himself was not able to fulfil this role, or because he had several armies operating simultaneously in several theatres.

A third group of trusted vassals including *hatamoto* served as staff officers in the lord's military headquarters (*honjin*). They were usually ranked as *bugyo* (commissioners). Bugyo often headed specific branches of the general administration of a fief such as finance chief (*kanjo-bugyo*), auditor (*kanjo-ginmi-yaku*), town administrator (*machi-bugyo*), or head of construction (*fushin-bugyo*). Since all civilian activities also served the military purposes of the lord, samurai were at the top of everything. There were also bugyo with purely military areas of responsibility such as armour (*gusoku-bugyo*), firearms (*teppo-bugyo*), bows and arrows (*yumiya-bugyo*), lances (*yari-bugyo*), or long pikes (*nagae-bugyo*). These officials were not only in charge of safekeeping and maintaining equipment but also of training soldiers in their use. In times of war these specialized officers served on the staff while the units they equipped and trained served in the field or as headquarter or castle protection troops.

A figure of great importance in many daimyos' military establishments was the *gun-bugyo*, alternatively known as *gunshi*, *sobugyo*, or *ikusa-bugyo*.

A Takeda Arquebus and Bow Unit

Mixed weapons missile units drawn up for battle were typically composed of a number of base units of five missile ashigaru with their own command element. Both bows and guns were included, but towards the end of the 16th and in the 17th century the number of guns exceeded the bows. As gun and bow troops were separately administered, it was of course also possible to field a large force of just one type.

In the Takeda army, each group of five missile ashigaru was led by a samurai ranked *keigo yoriki,* who had a horse and two personal retainers on foot holding the reins of his horse and carried his lance, spare sandals etc. In most other armies, the *keigo yoriki* mounted samurai with retainers was replaced by a single ashigaru corporal *(ko-gashira).*

In addition, there were also a number of support troops attached to this unit, tasked with providing ammunition to the missile ashigaru.

Becoming the commander of a larger unit (*ashigaru-daisho*) meant enhanced income and prestige for a samurai. This is expressed in his increased personal retinue of five men. Actually, the 46-strong Takeda army unit shown here could be subdivided into two different sub-units: 25 missile troops and 21 attack troops (mounted samurai with retainers on foot). This was one way the Takeda brought their superior cavalry strength to bear while not neglecting modern firepower.

Units like this were often positioned in front and at the flanks of field formations to shoot at attacking enemies to slow them down. The Takeda would place ashigaru units armed with long pikes (*nagae-yari*) in long, thin lines behind the missile troops to provide cover behind which the front line could withdraw before it was overrun by the enemy. The pike-armed troops would hold the attacking enemy, and foot samurai with shorter lances and/or mounted forces would counterattack.

Command Structure of a Takeda Bow & Gun Unit

1	Mounted commander *(ashigaru-daisho)*
2	Mounted officers *(keigo yoriki)*
3–5	Retainers
6	Lance carrier to 1 & 2
7	Horse handler *(kuchitori)*
8	Ashigaru *teppo* gunner
9	Ashigaru *yumi* bowman

Sections from the *Kawanakajima-kassen-zu* (see also p. 45)
Iwakuni Art Museum, Yamaguchi Prefecture

A pair of six-part painted folding screens showing scenes from the Fourth Battle of Kawanakajima in 1561. Archrivals Takeda Shingen and Uesugi Kenshin faced each other several times at Kawanakajima in Shinano Province (today´s Nagano Prefecture). Their Fourth Battle showed two brilliant samurai generals with their well-trained and highly motivated armies at their tactical best. The costly fight ended in a draw.

In his portrayals of Shingen´s headquarters and main unit and Yamagata Masakage´s troops the painter displays intimate knowledge of the Takeda military organisation. This detail shows a single row of ashigaru armed with long pikes, backed up by a double row of samurai and ashigaru with shorter lances. All officers are mounted and accompanied by personal retainers on foot.

(opposite page)
First Takeda Battle Line
The first battle line is formed by mixed missile units whose base are groups of three handgunners and two bowmen led by a mounted samurai with two retainers holding his horse´s reins and his lance. The picture below with its enlarged details indicates the samurai´s rank as *keigo (yoriki)*. The missile ashigaru are dressed in uniform armour from their lord´s arsenal, and have a variation of the Takeda diamond-like *kamon* painted in gold on their *jingasa* conical helmets.

The gunshi´s position was acquired purely on the base of a samurai´s individual talents and merits, and most gunshi did not come from top families and did not command a large body of their own men. One possible translation is "chief of general staff", similar in importance to that post in Prussian/German military history. The job included counselling the daimyo on even the most delicate matters, designing schemes and military strategies and preventing in a discreet way that young, inexperienced or incapable daimyo committed too many mistakes. There are several legendary gunshi in the history of Sengoku samurai, such as Yamamoto Kansuke (died in battle in 1561) who served Takeda Shingen, or Naoe Kanetsugu (1560–1620) who combined the post of gunshi with the position of karo. He served Uesugi Kagekatsu so well that he eventually received his own fief worth 300.000 *koku*, which made him equal in terms of income to some very influential daimyo.

Translating historical Japanese titles usually includes their interpretation, because different clans spread responsibilities in different ways, using differing labels. Often these positions have no equivalent in Western military history. The rank of *taisho* (*-daisho* in compound nouns) generally means an officer commanding a unit which could vary in size from a mere "platoon" to an entire army led by a *sodaisho*. A *samurai-daisho* was the commander of a major field unit whose sub-units were led by various specialized *taisho*, such as arquebusiers under a *teppo-daisho*, archers under a *yumi-daisho*, or lance-armed troops under *yari-daisho*. Ashigaru troops were usually administered separately from samurai troops and came under the orders of *ashigaru-daisho*, but there were also specialists like *ashigaru-teppo-daisho*, *ashigaru-nagaeyari-daisho* etc. These titles indicate the social rank of the troops as well as their specialization. Subalterns serving under the *taisho* class of officers were often known as *yoriki* (junior officers). All these officers were samurai and usually mounted, surrounded by a small number of their own retainers on foot. This gives a Sengoku army a very officer-heavy appearance: The Takeda household troops comprised about 30 *ashigaru-daisho* positions with 785 ashigaru under their command as well as 255 horsemen, which is peculiar to the Takeda and their cavalry-focused military organization. *Ashigaru-daisho* were expected to fight in the front lines.

As opposed to almost all *fudai* class ranks which were hereditary, positions such as *ashigaru-daisho* could be attained even by warriors of very humble origins through promotion. The famous gunshi Yamamoto Kansuke for instance came from an insignificant rural samurai family and entered the service of Lord Takeda Shingen through mediation from the *karo* Itagaki Nobutaka. He reached his position by rising through the ranks.

Other officers with tasks other than leading units of men were called *metsuke* or *kenshi* (provost). These were in charge of scouting, communications and worked in command and control as a kind of military police. These tasks were considered so important that they were overseen by a group of officers directly under the daimyo. Their job was to observe the performance of individual samurai and units, reporting to the lord. The intention was, apart from spurning the men to do their best at all times, to find out the best role and position for each part of the army and to make sure that rewards were given to the right men. These could comprise anything from *sake* to cash, but also arms and even full sets of armour. The HQ unit usually had positions for auxiliaries, who had to carry these rewards until they changed owners.

Turning to the equivalent of NCOs, there was the rank of *kashira* or *kumi-gashira* ("group leader"). Again, this could be specialized in *teppo-gashira, yumi-gashira, yari-gashira* (arquebus, bow, lance) etc. Holders of this rank were low-ranking samurai or veteran ashigaru in charge of a group of soldiers. They were supported by a number of "corporals", called *ko-gashira* ("ko" means small). As evidenced by pictorial sources, *ko-gashira* were typically in charge of squads of five missile ashigaru, either teppo- or bow-armed or mixed. That meant that missile units often had a larger number of officers and NCOs than all other unit types. As for the cavalry-heavy Takeda army, this rank was called *keigo-yoriki* and was held by a mounted samurai, not an ashigaru NCO on foot. Not unlike British sergeant-majors, Kashira- and ko-gashira-ranked soldiers often carried canes as symbols of their authority, and of course these came in handy when the need arose to show a man his place. Kashira sometimes wore their own individual *sashimono* identifying flag or object on the back of their armour, or the same as their men, or none at all.

Feudal Samurai Service and Professional Troops in Garrisons

In order to be able to afford his equipment, a horse, and to employ a few personal retainers a samurai either held land from his lord *(chigyochi)* or was supported by direct payments *(horoku)*, which meant a mix of classical feudal obligations and modern economic influences. Until the final third of the 16th century many samurai actually lived on their lands which were inside the territory of a daimyo. Along with some members of the village elders class they were considered *jizamurai* ("rural warriors"). It was Hideyoshi who took away arms from the non-samurai rural population and phased out the practice of countryside-based part-time samurai.

The period of transition between the older practice described above and the newer trend to have samurai live permanently removed from their lands in or close to the lord's castles is highlighted by the case of Okamoto Masahide, a member of the Hojo daimyos' mounted bodyguard (see pp. 35, 45 & 47). Okamoto's family lived on his lands, but he himself spent longer periods of time in the capital Odawara to perform his responsibilities. He even maintained a house in Odawara. If an army such as that of the Hojo clan was needed for warfare, all that could be done very quickly was to call up the ashigaru household troops living in garrisons and those samurai with their retainers who lived in or close to the capital. Further contingents *(shu)* included the *jizamurai* living across the territory. These were called up in their districts and gathered under a banner of their own before joining the main army. The typical pattern was that rural samurai from a certain district rushed to the castle which controlled it, ready to man a fortification or to be sent to fight elsewhere. Besides joining the army when called up, local samurai were also responsible for keeping their district's castles in a state of defensibility and manning them when needed. In addition, district borders needed to be kept safe and general administrative tasks performed. In the Sengoku Period outer castles were often just simple affairs constructed of wood and earth on flattened hilltops which did not require a substantial permanent garrison and did not offer room for one (on fortifications, see volume 2). A mostly part-time force was sufficient to defend them.

This feudal organization of a large proportion of samurai service cost precious time at the time of mobilization. Other disadvantages included imbalances in troop types and quality as well as a lack of opportunity to train together in large formations. It became a hallmark of a successfully expanding daimyo at the end of the late Sengoku Period that he became capable of maintaining ever increasing proportions of his army in his growing main castles and castle towns. Freed them from their rural tasks, his samurai could spend more time on their army training and concentrate on their job in the military. Therefore more and more of the lord's fighting men permanently turned into professional soldiers, ready to serve at a moment's notice. First, this tendency affected elite troops directly serving the daimyo such as Okamoto Masahide, with the rural samurai being the last to change their way of life and service. The background of this development was an improving economic situation and lords' ability to participate in the profits traders, farmers, and craftsmen made. The result was the establishment of a growing core of military professionals living in or close to the main castles who were ready to fight any time. Main castles served as massive depots stockpiling supplies for months; whole armies could be outfitted quickly. Improved roads and transportation meant that armies and supplies could move faster and further. However, there were daimyo who adhered to the old "backwoods" model with their farmer-samurai armies, such as the Chosokabe family (see pp. 66–68). This was enough for them to conquer most of isolated, quiet Shikoku, but once the mighty military machine of Toyotomi Hideyoshi landed in 1585 the Chosokabe were simply swept away.

One consequence of the enlargement of army cores was the corresponding enlargement of major castles and their towns *(jokamachi)*. Ashigaru typically dwelt in long wooden barrack buildings, *nagaya*, without a family of their own (and dreamt of a great career including social and financial advances). Samurai typically lived in their own town quarters in small houses with small gardens for one family *(buke-yashiki)* provided by the lord. Promotions and a rise in the ranks often meant a move into a bigger house in the same castle town. Along with their incomes the number of personal retainers and horses a lucky samurai had would rise accordingly. Besides service as guards, escorts and in administrative duties, daily routines included individual and unit-based military exercises.

STRENGTH AND COMPOSITION OF ARMIES

Regarding the general development of the strength of armies during the course of the 16th and early 17th centuries there is a clear tendency of increasing troop numbers. Primarily this was caused by the process of political concentration taking place in that period, which meant that big fish were constantly eating small fish and incorporating their former territories into their own increasing lands. Land was given as fiefs to samurai, so taking over a new district or province meant acquiring new fighting men as well, unless they were all dispossessed and made to go, thus becoming *ronin* (masterless samurai). For these traditional parts of a daimyo´s army the military obligation remained more or less the same during the Sengoku Period: Senior vassals had to field about 300 men per 10.000 koku of income, in the Edo Period this rose slightly to an average of about 350 men. However, daimyo managed to increase their own income significantly and became able to maintain more "household" troops under their very own banner, which strengthened their position also in the face of their vassals. Furthermore, alliances became more large-scale (such as the Oda-Tokugawa liaison lasting from the 1560´s until Nobunaga´s death in 1582), which meant fielding larger armies including allied troops became a possibility. Oda Nobunaga would most likely not have won the crucial battle of the Anagawa in 1570 without the efforts provided by Tokugawa Ieyasu´s large contingent. On the other hand, Ieyasu lost to Takeda Shingen at Mikatagahara in 1573 when he only had the support of a 3000-men contingent from Nobunaga.

The topic of troop strength was crucial in a "civil war" situation in which opposing armies frequently were very similar in their composition including specific capabilities and shortcomings. Having higher numbers on the battlefield was the easiest way to gain an advantage. For instance, Tokugawa Ieyasu scored his three crucial victories in 1600, 1614/15 and 1615 on his way to supreme power by making increasingly superior numbers tell (see table on opposite page). There were two major battles where he was outnumbered – Mikatagahara in 1573 (1:3) and Komaki-Nagakute in 1584 (estimated at up to 1:5). Both times Ieyasu had no choice but to make a stand.

Ieyasu lost the first battle and scored a draw in the second, which earned him much respect. Ieyasu´s opponent at Komaki-Nagakute, Toyotomi Hideyoshi, was neither a daredevil nor a tactical genius, but a master of strategy and diplomacy. He basically never fought without a significant superiority in numbers

Oda Nobunaga, the third of Japan's great unifiers, preferred a markedly different strategy, fighting with much smaller numerical advantages and even when outnumbered. He did not share in the ambition to surround enemies strategically and persuade them to join him; Nobunaga was keen on quashing his enemies. He was ready to accept losses on a large scale as he knew conquests would swell his ranks. In 1560 he won one of the most spectacular victories of his age by attacking Imagawa Yoshimoto with a mere 3000 men. His opponent´s strength has been estimated at 15,000–30,000. While Hideyoshi initiated the fighting in only 46.8% of his battles, Nobunaga did so in 70.5%. Hideyoshi died peacefully in 1598 in his castle, Nobunaga was murdered by a discontent vassal.

How were Sengoku Period armies up to the early 17th c. composed? It is clear that the number of troops fighting on foot, especially ashigaru, increased over the decades. The number or percentage of samurai fighting on horseback, however, decreased. In the late 16th century, many samurai fought on foot, which would have been very rare in preceding centuries. Half or more of all soldiers now carried a lance *(yari)* as their main weapon. Among missile-armed troops the number of *teppo* handgunners often increased at the expense of archers, but fluctuations in the availability of guns and supplies made this trend uneven. The larger trend is documented in table 3 on p. 44 which introduces us to the samurai Tomioka Hidetomo of Koizumi Castle. He had to supply troops to his daimyo Hojo Ujiyasu as part of Kozuke Province´s contingent in 1559. The table includes two different contributions to the Hojo army from 1572 and 1581 as well as Honda Minbuzaemon´s unit in the service of the Sakai daimyo family, recorded in 1700 (see pp. 69–72 for a graphic representation of Honda´s unit).

The core of the first three units from the late 16th c. are still groups of mounted samurai with their retainers on foot, just as in previous centuries. However, these are now supplemented by large numbers of lance-armed ashigaru and smaller squads of mixed missile troops. The Hojo were not at the forefront of military innovation in this period, and other major daimyo such as the Takeda and the Mori expected their vassals to bring more handgunners and archers. Towards the end of our period, and fully visible in 1700, the number of cavalry decreased, half of the samurai now serving dismounted. *Zohyo Monogatari* had, in mid-17th century, stated that fighting on horseback "has been out of use for a long time." (p. 53). Finally, cavalry was now only one troop type among others, but with dwindling relevance.

Honda´s unit from 1700 is markedly different from units of similar numbers during the Sengoku Period. It also reflects the increased desire for more comfort in peaceful times. The formerly numerous force of ashigaru with lances has been cut, and support troops massively increased. Furthermore, guns were now available in much greater quantities and outnumber bows several times over.

Strength of Opposing Armies

Table 1: Tokugawa Ieyasu and Opponents

Battle / Campaign	Ieyasu	Opponent
Sekigahara 1600	90.000–100.000 (further increased by turncoats from the Western Army)	80.000 (Western Army under Ishida Mitsunari)
Osaka Winter 1614/15	164.000	113.000 (Toyotomi)
Osaka Summer 1615	150.000	60.000 (Toyotomi)

Table 2: Toyotomi Hideyoshi and Opponents

Battle / Campaign	Hideyoshi	Opponents	Ratio of Strength
Tottori Castle 1580	20.000	4.000 (Kikkawa Tsuneie)	10 : 2
Takamatsu Castle 1582	30.000	5.000 (Shimizu Muneharu)	10 : 1,7
Yamazaki 1582	27.000	13.000 (Akechi Mitsuhide)	10 : 4,8
Shizugatake 1583	30.000	20.000 (Shibata Katsuie)	10 : 6,7
Komaki-Nagakute 1584	100.000	20.000 (Tokugawa Ieyasu)	10 : 2
Ota Castle 1585	60.000	5.000 (Ota Munemasa)	10 : 0,8
Takajo 1587	90.000	20.000 (Shimazu Iehisa)	10 : 2,2
Odawara Castle 1590	220.000	56.000 (Hojo Ujimasa, Ujinao)	10 : 2,5

Souces: Senryaku Senjutsu Heiki, vol. 1, p. 41 and Wiki: Takajo.

Troop Types:	Tomioka Hidetomo 1559	Miyagi 1572	Ikeda Sozaemon 1581	Honda Minbuzaemon, c. 1700
Mounted Samurai	60	80	70	31
Foot Samurai	-	-	-	33
Ashigaru with Lance/Pike	100	170	120	30
Archers	20	10	10	19
Arquebus handgunners	20	20	10	72
Other ashigaru	50	50 plus 30 carriers of flags	60	55
Personal retainers (porters, horse handlers etc.)	50	unknown	unknown	131
Supply and baggage train	No data (farmers pressed into service?)	unknown	unknown	10
Total	300 plus supports	360 plus supports	270 plus supports	381

Table 3: Troop Types in Various Contingents

Note: Troop numbers for Tomioka, Miyagi, and Ikeda are extrapolated because of the smaller size of their contingents.
Source: Senryaku Senjutsu Heiki, vol.1, p. 76-7.; Conlan, p. 134-5.; Turnbull: Samurai Armies 1467–1649, p. 25.

Mounted samurai charging with cloth *horo* on their backs.

The *horo* enlarges the physical appearance of a warrior considerably, despite only being a piece of cloth on a wicker frame. This improved their visibility as messengers *(tsukai-ban)* but could also intimidate opponents on foot who were attacked by horo wearers (Still from the movie "Sekigahara", 2017). For details on *horo* see pp. 92 & 103.

ARMY DIVISIONS AND TROOP TYPES

Samurai Cavalry: Myth and Reality – The Takeda Re-Examined

In many pre-modern societies, mounted warriors were members of a social and military elite. Most other warriors/soldiers fought on foot and were at a disadvantage against mounted men, unless they were very well organized, disciplined and equipped with the right mix of polearms and missile weapons. This is not only valid for much of Medieval and Early Modern Europe, but also for the earlier part of Japanese military history. Impressive images such as those from Kurosawa Akira's famous 1980 movie "Kagemusha" show dense formations of samurai cavalry *(kiba-gundan)* as swift and deadly shock troops, and it took a technological and tactical revolution to stop them. This refers of course to the re-creation of the famous Takeda cavalry attack at Nagashino in 1575. The Oda foot soldiers that stopped the cavalry in the movie were all armed with arquebus and drawn up in three ranks behind a strong wooden fence.

However, archaeological discoveries in Japan yield a very different picture. If one includes an examination of pictorial and text sources it becomes clear that the true military role and the battlefield value of samurai cavalry in the late 16th and early 17th centuries has been overestimated, even glorified. Few samurai armies of this period contained more than 10% mounted troops. For example, the Uesugi in 1575, the year of the battle of Nagashino, had this proportion of mounted men (including all mounted officers commanding foot troops) in various sub-units of their army: 40 mounted men out of 375; 20 out of 250; 8 out of 81; 5 out of 52. The percentage of mounted samurai of 16% and 20% achieved in Akechi Mitsuhide's army in 1581 and by the later Hojo lords is already above average. Cavalry was costly, so during the Edo Period (1603–1867) the number of horsemen further declined. The Matsuura clan army, based at Hirado in Kyushu, had only 20 mounted men among 650 according to a record painted in 1796 (the plan executed and illustrated then actually dates back to late-17th century ideas developed by the strategist Yamaga Soko, who also designed Hirado Castle). The famous exception was the Takeda army until 1582, which could field up to 30% of its strength as mounted samurai, the premier mounted force of its age, but also one of its spectacular losers.

Mounted samurai fulfilled various roles in the army. They acted as scouts and messengers *(tsukai-ban)* and served as commanders and sub-commanders of units across the army. Respected mounted samurai held positions as *kenshi* and *metsuke* (supervisors, provosts).

All mounted samurai were accompanied by at least one retainer on foot who had to hold the horse's reins, carry his master's weapons, helmet, or spare straw sandals for horse and rider (straw horse sandals replaced iron horseshoes in Japan). These support troops were often called *wakato*. Many samurai had more than one servant on foot. Taking Okamoto Masahide's 14 retainers on foot as an example (see pp. 46–47), several of these would accompany him directly into battle, while the remainder, especially the six ashigaru armed with long pikes, would join specialized units led by somebody other than their master. Those who had their hands free to draw their sword or fight with a yari *(yariwaki)* would usually join in a charge, while others holding their masters' weapons and other equipment would stay behind or follow more slowly.

Okamoto served in the mounted lifeguards of his daimyo *(umawari-shu)*, so his normal position on the battlefield and on the march would be close to headquarters. Such units were not mere bodyguards but were regularly used to ride decisive charges and inspire others by their hard fighting.

Other mounted elements included all high-ranking samurai, and the staff officers. These joined the lord inside the HQ area surrounded by cloth curtains *(maku)* and left their horses with their personal retainers outside.

The best pictorial sources to study the various functions and positions held by mounted samurai in the Takeda army are the so-called *Kawanakajima-kassen-zu* in the Iwakuni Art Museum (see pp. 38–39). These are a pair of 16th c. painted screens once used to divide interior spaces. Each screen measures about 550 x 150 cm and shows one complete unit of the Takeda army deployed for battle during the Fourth Battle of Kawanakajima in 1561. Realism and attention to the smallest detail down to the least important members of the army make these screens outstanding sources. It becomes evident that all mounted samurai served in the roles described above; there were none left to form independent cavalry units except for the lifeguards. This excludes for Japan the existence of strong regiments or brigades of line cavalry as we see them in European armies, possibly peaking in the Age of Napoleon. Mounted samurai were mainly officers to foot units. Although there were many such officers, the only available unit of massed, dedicated cavalry was the lord's elite umawari-shu, rarely more than the equivalent of a European squadron.

One reason for this striking difference is to be found in the different social status of a mounted warrior in feudal Japan and a regular cavalryman in, again, France under Napoleon. A samurai, even if he did not own a horse, was a member of an elite, the gentry, and enjoyed high social prestige, whereas European cavalrymen were, apart from some of their officers, sons of farmers, artisans and tradesmen just like most other soldiers in the army. Europeans in regular cavalry units did not personally own their horse or equipment, but the mounted samurai supplied and owned everything as their personal properties. Moreover, samurai took great pride in assembling an impressive group of followers on foot to support them and show off the status of their master. This meant that "cavalry" units included more men on foot than mounted. With only one man among several in a such a unit actually fighting on horseback, the Japanese system was less efficient than the European system, which was able to produce a larger number of prime combatants on horseback. When proceeding to the attack, mounted samurai and their retainers on foot banded together, forming mixed groups in the old Japanese style. Often relatives or neighbours from the same area stayed close to each other. The foot retainers tried to stay close to their masters at all times, including charge and melee. Not all of them had a helmet or a complete suit of armour, or even half-armour. They wore what was available, but all were armed at least with a short sword in their belt, while some had standard *katana* swords or polearms. Even camp tools could be used as weapons.

Once the attack was ordered, horsemen and foot soldiers moved out at a high pace. Men running on foot tried to keep up with the horses, which naturally tended to be faster. After a while a thin screen of horsemen was ahead of a larger group of hard-running retainers. The spectacular helmets and back flags *(sashimono)* of the leading samurai provided important, easily visible clues to their retainers, who tried to catch up with their masters to be able to help in the fight. The Ii clan had a system of identifying their mounted samurai, which maintained clan uniformity, but also allowed for individual recognition. It was a red sashimono flag for all, with the individual's name written in striking gold letters, and a personal coat of arms *(kamon)* added by some.

In stark contrast to the tactics used before the 15th century, when noble samurai challenged each other and shot arrows from a distance, Sengoku tactics emphasized fast and furious attacks by mounted men, followed by more on foot trying to engage in close-quarter combat as soon as possible, not least because this reduced the impact of the enemy's missile troops. The first wave to hit the enemy was the relatively small group of horsemen. The Takeda's advantage lay in the larger number of their mounted samurai, which meant that the impact of their first wave was bigger. With three times more mounted men available than to an enemy of equal numbers, chances grew that the Takeda could overwhelm opposition quickly.

In accordance to changing tactics the weaponry used by mounted samurai had also changed. A pair of swords or *tachi* sword and dagger were their secondary armament, whereas a short to medium-length, sturdy *yari* (lance) was the main weapon. Some yari for mounted warfare were just about a man's height, others between 2.4 and 3.6 metres long. This weapon was very well balanced and extremely versatile in trained hands.

Case Study: Okamoto Hachirozaemon Masahide, a mid-ranking Samurai serving the Hojo of Odawara

Okamoto was a *hatamoto* and a member of the *umawari-shu*, which was an elite unit of 94, later 120 mounted mid-ranking samurai directly serving Lord Hojo. Okamoto lived off his fief at Yoshioka (today's Kanagawa Prefecture, then Sagami Province) with had an annual yield of 59 *kan'mon* (i.e. *koku*: one koku being the amount of rice needed to feed one man for one year). In addition to this, he received a stipend for his military service in the horse guards. Any surplus rice could be converted into money or used to buy goods or services. Okamoto had a second house in the capital, Odawara. There is a preserved letter from the daimyo, Hojo Ujiyasu (1515–1571), to his vassal which gives us precise information as to what military contribution Okamoto was expected to make.

The document asks for 15 military men to turn out for service, which seems to have included a formal parade: one of the men had to be mounted (*kiba* – Okamoto himself), plus 4 foot samurai *(kachi)*, and 10 foot soldiers *(ashigaru)*. All names and the order of march are given. First on parade was Shirozaemon, the banner bearer (as opposed to samurai, ashigaru did not have family names yet), to be followed by Genjuro, an ashigaru with back flag and sword. Next were six ashigaru with long pikes (which measured only 3.6 m in the Hojo army). Their names were Genshiro, Heishiro, Yogoro, San'nyu, Emonshiro, and Tojiro. Then came Okamoto himself, on a horse that was to be armoured in gold for the parade (horse armour usually was not made of metal but of textiles, leather, and papier mâché). In front of and behind Okamoto there were pairs of foot samurai with back flags, named Take Shozaemon, Suzuki Han'emon, Sugiyama Sojiro, and Oba Yashichiro. Bringing up the rear were two more ashigaru, called Tarogoro and Sei'emon, who carried swords and perhaps Okamoto's additional equipment.

A foot samurai enjoyed an annual income of 5, an ashigaru 2.5 *kan´mon*. There is a conspicuous omission in the document: Okamoto is not supposed to bring or did not bring any archers or handgunners which drew critique in another letter. It found further fault with the fact that the colour of Okamoto´s ashigaru armour did not match the colour of the units they were to be parading or fighting with. Apparently, unit distinction within the Hojo army included foot soldiers´ armour colours. As it was Okamoto who had to lend them their armour, it was his fault not to have had them re-lacquered in time for service (cf. Conlan, p. 130).

Okamato and his Retinue on Parade
1 Shirozaemon leading the procession, carrying Okamoto´s banner
2 Genjuro is an ashigaru with *sashimono* back flag and sword
3 Six ashigaru armed with long pikes (length only 3.6 m in the Hojo clan)
4 Okamoto himself on his horse, which wears golden horse armour for the parade
5 2 x 2 foot samurai *(kachi)* with back flags walking before and behind their master
6, 7 Two ashigaru with swords (no lances) serving as horse-driver and Okamoto´s lance bearer
8 Not mentioned in the source, but certainly needed for a campaign was a number of servants and hired men to carry baggage and provisions

Contemporary pictorial sources indicate that marching two abreast was standard practice for foot soldiers.

A note on the banners displayed: Okamoto´s personal sashimono shows not his personal mon but that belonging to his unit, the *umawari-shu* (mounted lifeguards). Some of his men also display the Hojo mon, but on a yellow sashimono. The five-coloured large *nobori* rectangular flag was used by units of banner signallers in the Hojo army.

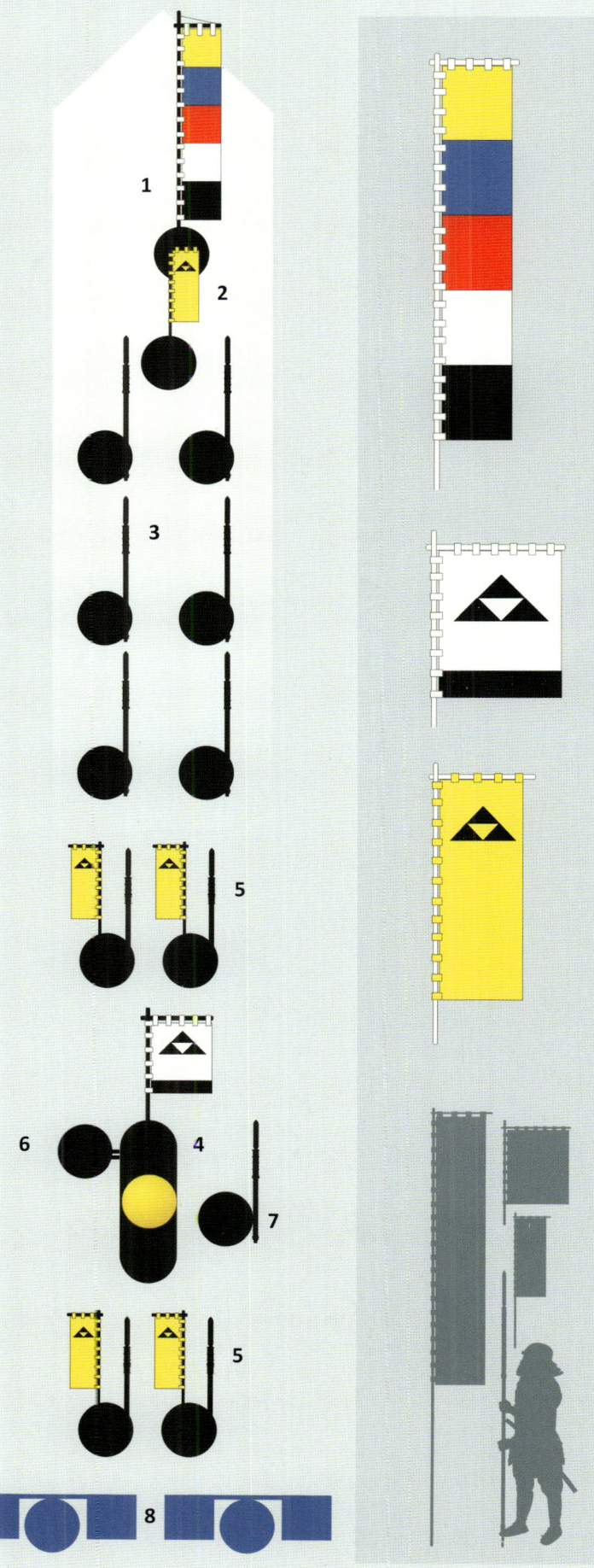

Japanese Horses

Japan´s historical horse population is only survives in small numbers in remote areas such as mountains or islands. After the Meiji Restoration Japan preferred larger horse breeds imported from abroad. This horse belongs to a population of 130 animals who live half-wild on the Southern island of Yonaguni in Okinawa Prefecture. Okinawa´s predecessor, the Ryukyu Kingdom, is noted for having exported horses to China as early as the 14th century.

Depending on the owner´s preferences, there were various lengths and forms of blades, which were usually both suitable for thrusting and slashing. However, the 17th century handbook *Zohyo Monogatari* mentions a samurai using a hooked yari on horseback, hitting his own mount in the eye, so it discourages using hooked blades when mounted. The yari was wielded with one, preferably two hands from the saddle. Many suits of armour have small metal rings attached to the breastplate. These were for securing the horse´s reins so that the lance could be wielded with both hands. The horse was now controlled by movements of the body and especially the knees. A good warhorse was expected to react instinctively to these touches.

The traditional main weapon, the longbow and the large quiver necessary, were of little or no use for this kind of combat, they even would impede movement. The rider had to be able to swirl his lance freely around and over his entire body. This is why the bow in this period was relegated to dedicated units of foot soldiers and perhaps a few high-ranking, nostalgic samurai who could afford a retainer to carry the extra weapon for them, just in case an opportunity to use it arose. This was of course a demonstration of social status and individuality rather than an important military contribution. Archery did not die out however, it was still useful to cover units of teppo handgunners during the lengthy period of reloading, and it was also used in small-scale and in siege combat in the Sengoku Period. Japanese mounted archery has survived to this day in the *yabusame* rituals, performed at Shinto shrines and preserved mostly through the efforts of the Ogasawara family, whose ancestors were daimyo in the Sengoku Period.

By the 16th century there were many different types of armour for different forms of combat available to European men-at-arms, especially different equipment for mounted and dismounted combat. In Japan there were not many differences between samurai armour for mounted and dismounted fighting. The way the *tachi* sword was mounted by riders was noted above, as were the small rings on the breastplate to tie the reins to. The other difference was the addition of *haidate*, a large but flexible pair of armour plates suspended from the hip, protecting the upper legs under the *kusazuri* skirts of the main armour. Haidate are not a pleasure to wear when walking, but they helped to protect a vulnerable area of the mounted samurai. There were also fashionable suits of armour for horses as mentioned in the Okamoto case study, but most historians agree that these were mostly reserved for parades because they were heavy and cumbersome in combat. The same seems to be true for horse face masks, called *bamen*, even though these had been known since the Kofun Period (3rd to 6th centuries).

Saddle and Stirrups

Historical saddlery from Japan, including a pair of iron stirrups *(abumi)* which could be used to kick enemies on foot during a melee.

Mounted samurai were dangerous opponents for fighters on foot isolated from their units or taken by surprise. Being attacked by a mounted man was frightening enough, but the effect was still aggravated by the demonic face masks, elaborate helmets and colourful banners many samurai wore. If no tight unit of pike-armed troops or field fortifications were close by to provide protection, mounted charges had to be absorbed by troops on foot who were likely to take casualties. Daring foot soldiers tried to cut the horses' reins to take away much of the riders control over their mounts. To counter this ancient combat tactic samurai wrapped layers of thick cotton cloth around the leather reins. These lengths of cloth were often dyed in alternating colours (white, red, blue etc.) and were a typical feature of a samurai horse ready for battle. Fighters on foot aimed at surrounding a mounted samurai and pulling him from his horse to stab him. To enable pulling, some yari had one or two small cross blades or hooks, and there were specialized polearms and grappling weapons including ropes with weights to be thrown over the opponent. While a fully-armed mounted samurai was generally well-protected, his arm and knee pits offered targets for thrusting weapons. However, this was a dangerous enterprise as the horseman moved quickly and was able to cover a 360-degree arc with his razor-sharp yari which gave him a striking reach of several metres in all directions. A hit with a yari conducted with full force from overhead was likely to cause a disabling injury even through light armour. Of course, it was important for the mounted samurai to have his retainers on foot catching up soon to help him against enemies surrounding him or cover him in case he was wounded.

There were other options to stop a mounted attack, including to launch a counter attack by one's own mounted troops. Generally, formations were much less rigid and not as deep as in Europe at the time, and various well-developed communication systems (see pp. 63–66) enabled commanders to react swiftly by sending columns on horse or on foot to crucial points of the fight or to hit an attacker in the flank.

In the second half of the 16th century yet another option to break the power of mounted samurai (and their followers on foot) became increasingly apparent: The matchlock arquebus (*teppo* or *tanegashima*, see pp. 58–62). For this, gunners needed to be massed to form firing lines with devastating fire power which combined the effects of the projectile with noise, smoke, and smell. It was probably the mostly non-samurai Ikko-ikki rebels who for the first time employed these tactics in Japan – against none less than mighty Oda Nobunaga. Nobunaga was inspired to gather 3000 (other sources indicate only 1000) gunners in three ranks behind a wooden palisade on the battlefield of Nagashino in 1575. Used in this way, his men could fire salvoes of hundreds of bullets with only short intervals because loading time was cut down to one third. Still, archaeological findings proved that even this fire power did not destroy the Takeda attack completely as suggested in Kurosawa's film. It only brought disorder and hesitation to the charge, and one should not overlook that there was also a small river running just in front of the palisades. Much of the killing was done by lance- and sword-armed Oda samurai who sallied out through small gaps in the palisades and cut down the stunned attackers. There was yet another major difference between Japanese *kiba-gundan* and European cavalry: The horses themselves. The historical Japanese horse had been genetically influenced by the Mongol horse and had grown into an original race. Since 1988, the skeleton of Takeda Shingen's own horse has been on display at Fujimura Memorial Hall in Kofu, the Takeda's old capital in Kai Province (Yamanashi Prefecture). Shingen died in 1573 and his favourite horse's remains were found buried with honours. A study of its teeth revealed that it had been regularly fed with high-quality fodder. The horse had clearly been treated with respect. It stood a mere 120 cm tall, weighing around 250 kg (a modern racing horse is around 160 cm and 500 kg). Tsukahara Bokuden speaks of 129 cm as minimum horse size but warns against using horses that are too tall because these tended to be weak.

A Mounted Attack against Troops on Foot

The charging samurai are followed by their retainers on foot trying to catch up with their masters. The attacked army has already withdrawn its first line of foot troops, who have fired bows and guns at the attackers and caused some casualties. The second line of defence is a single row of ashigaru with long pikes (*nagae-yari*). These are kneeling, having rammed their pikes into the ground to hold them firmly against the attackers to break the impact of the charge. Directly behind them a long row of samurai with medium-length lances has moved up. It is their task to stab at any enemy penetrating the barrier of long pikes, and to be ready to sally out to enter close-quarter fighting.

A Reenactor at the Fourth Battle of Kawanakajima 1561
Shingen-ko Festival at Isawa-Onsen, Yamanashi Prefecture 2002

Note the two small rings attached to the breastplate, now decorated with silk tassels. Such rings could be used in battle to tie the horse's reins to them so that the rider had both hands free to wield his lance. Another usage for these rings was to pass through them a line that stabilized a sashimono (back flag) on the samurai's armoured back.

Yari: Pikes and Lances

A Pikes (nagae-yari) Used by Various Clans

1. Uesugi
2. Toyotomi
3. Oda
4. Hojo
5. Tokugawa
6. Takeda
7. Date

Compare scale at the right. Typical Japanese men of the period stood about 150 cm tall. Typical pike lengths as well as blade shapes and sashimono flags are well-documented. Most blades for ashigaru units were without hooks or guards. **Fig. 14** illustrates the full length of the part of the blade that was inside the lance.

B Blades, Various Variants
8. Sharpened bamboo lance
9. Composition of a yari: **9a:** Metal rings (*suji-gane*) reenforcing the shaft (*nakae*) in those parts that are subjected to heavy stress. The shaft is partly bound in rattan and lacquered for protection from the elements. **9b:** *ishizuki*, bottom end of the shaft, usually made of iron.
10–18 Classical, straight yari blades (*su-yari*) were similar to a shortened version of the archaic Japanese sword. They were double-edged and could have hooks (*kama-yari*, **16–17**) or come in fork-shape (*karimata*, **11**). *Yumonji-yari* (**14**) had hooks that were almost as long as the top. Extra-long blades were called *omi-yari* (**12**). **Fig. 13** is a blade protector (*saya*) made of wood and leather.

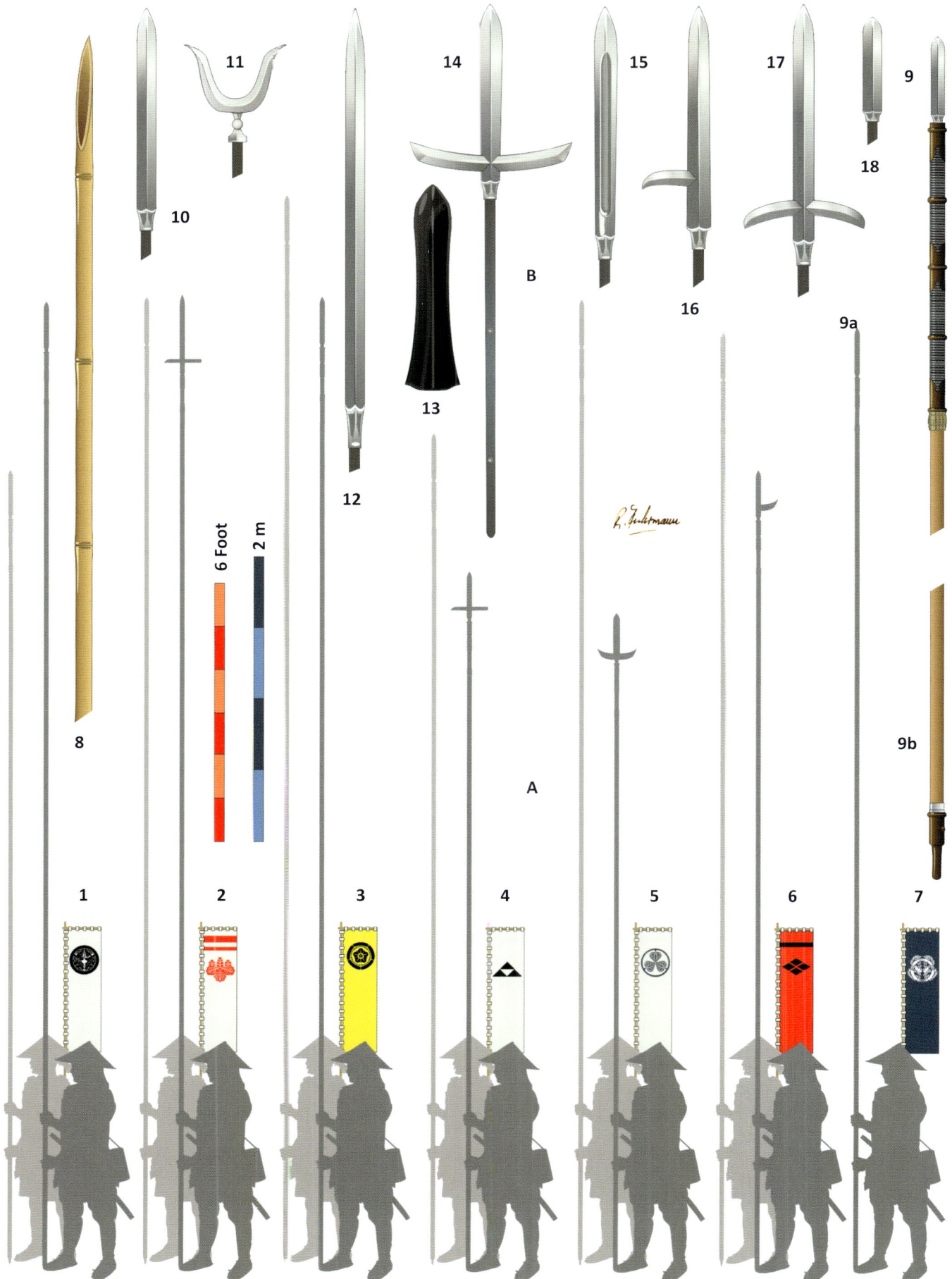

Lances (*yari*) stored in a rack on a castle wall
Main Tower of Himeji Castle

Castles also served as important arsenals. The lances shown here are relatively short, which would be useful when fighting inside buildings. Their blade is longer than most pikes produced for ashigaru, and their blood runnel is painted red.

The small size is most impressive when comparing the weights samurai and race horses had/have to carry. The samurai horse had to carry an armoured and armed samurai with a total weight of around 80 kg, approximately one third of its own weight. The race horse has to carry a small man in lightweight clothing weighing perhaps 1/6 or 1/7 its own weight. In addition to the rider and his gear, samurai horses were often covered with thick protective tassels back and front, wore a tall saddle with a wooden saddletree and stirrups made of lacquered wood or iron. It is obvious that heavily burdened samurai horses on their short legs are unlikely to have been very fast in the attack; most likely they barely outpaced the running foot retainers. When it came to the moment of physical impact against enemy troops these horses lacked the weight, mass, and size that characterized European shock cavalry such as cuirassiers or other heavy horse. Casting his European eye on Japanese horses in 1585, the Jesuit Luis Frois had no time for them: "While our horses are quite handsome, Japanese horses are inferior to them. Ours are able to immediately stop in their movements; theirs are very badly disciplined" (quoted after Kulturgegensätze, p. 196-205). Frois went on to comment on further differences in stable management, horse furniture, and care. He also observed differences such as the Japanese mounting their horses starting with the right leg, not the left one as Europeans did. Almost three centuries later the correspondent of the Illustrated London News complained:

"I have now ridden, or rather sat, upon seventy six horses, all horrible. They all stumble. The loins of some are higher than their shoulders, so that one slips forwards, and the backbones of all are ridgy. Their hind feet grow into points which turn up, and their hind legs all turn outwards, like those of a cat, from carrying heavy burdens at an early age. The same thing gives them a roll in their gait, which is increased by their awkward shoes." (ILN, August 17, 1861 – "Awkward shoes" is a reference to the horses' straw sandals.)

These unfavourable characteristics of Japanese horses explain why mounted samurai were almost never without supporters on foot holding the reins of their mounts. Frois observed: "When riding without retainers, riders have to take their horses' reins with both hands as opposed to just one as in Europe." For long-distance travel a palanquin (*kago*) carried by servants was preferred by those who had the right and the means to use one. This even seems to have caused even scenes of congestion, leading Toyotomi Hideyoshi to publish a written ban on palanquins in Osaka in 1595. The only exceptions allowed were elderly courtiers, senior religious dignitaries, and Tokugawa Ieyasu, Maeda Toshiie, Uesugi Kagekatsu, Mori Terumoto, and Kobayakawa Takekage, the most prominent among the princes of the realm.

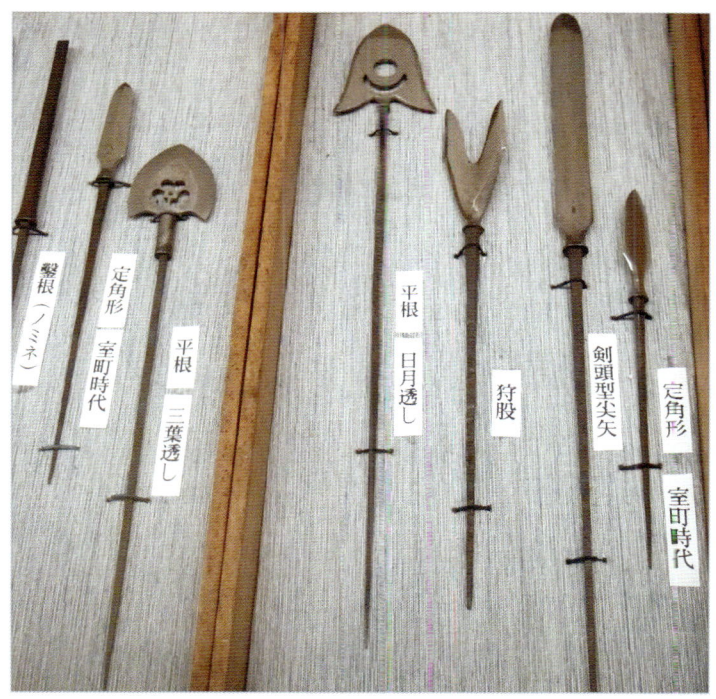 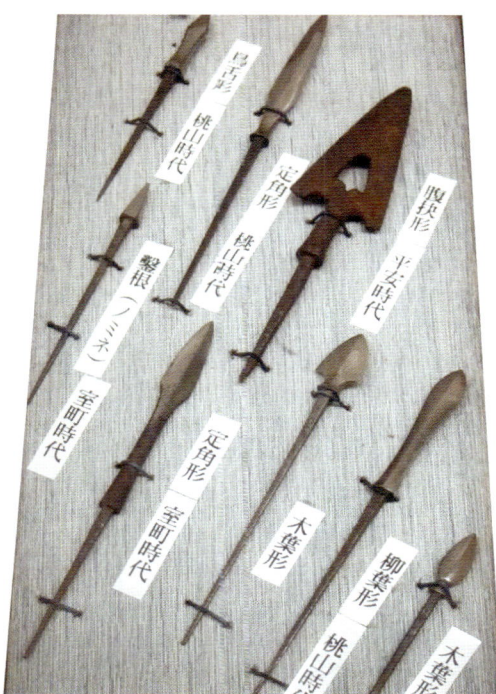

Arrowheads *Takeda Shrine, Kofu, Yamanashi Pref.*

Long before the Sengoku Period many different shapes of arrowheads had evolved. These were usually named after their function, e.g. "far-flying", "armour-piercing", "incendiary" or signalling by emitting whistling noises.

Among other daimyo only those above 50 and sick men were allowed to use palanquins, but only when travelling more than 1 *ri* (approx. 4 km). Japanese horses surely were not easy to control.

Certainly, horsemanship in Japan did not match that on display in certain cultures of continental North-East Asia. Owning and mounting a horse brought respect and status, but superlative riding skills did not play as high a role as elsewhere. However, a samurai could hope for a few other qualities in his horse which Frois, a man of the church, overlooked. For combat both mounted and on foot, agility and the ability to move fast were seen as a better protection than heavy armour. The samurai's little horse allowed his master to remain highly maneuverable while still affording him a certain advantage in height and mass against opponents on foot. Even the heavy stirrups (*abumi*) were utilized in the fight to kick enemies or to stand upright in them while whirling the lance. Basically, the horse was used as a moveable platform from which the samurai fought with his weapons against other warriors – the same principle that guided contemporary warship construction as well. The horse did not even have to be too fast in the attack as that would have delayed the arrival of the followers on foot on the scene.

Japanese horses were extremely resilient as demonstrated by pack horses weighing a mere 250 kg which were able to carry loads of up to 150 kg on daily marches of between 24 and 40 km. As no donkeys or mules were available in Japan, and mountainous roads limited the use of carts and wagons, the horse was of prime importance as a means of transport of men and supplies. Because they were small, Japanese horses needed less fodder than European horses which made them easier and cheaper to keep. Obviously, their large heads, short legs and round bellies did not make them visually attractive, but their qualities made them ideal for daimyo like Takeda Shingen, whose lands were in the mountainous Japanese Alps region. His horses were able to manage slopes of up to 30%. The *Bo-michi*, his main military trunk road connecting the capital Kofu with the Northern province of Shinano, which was frequently threatened by Uesugi Kenshin, was mostly only a path crossing wooded mountains, with a width of only 80 cm in parts. Small and sturdy horses were just right to navigate such roads.

Some daimyo were known for their own schools of horse-breeding. Among them were the Imagawa in the flatland province of Suruga on the Pacific coast, and the Tokugawa in neighboring Mikawa. Takeda horses however, known because of their typical dark brown colour as *Kai no kurokouma* ("small dark horses from Kai"), were bred in a much more challenging, harsher environment. They were small, but tough. Difficult natural surroundings increased their ability to adapt to circumstances as well as their intelligence. Unfortunately, the Takeda school of horse-breeding does not exist anymore and many of its secrets have been lost. We know that their horses were grown and trained in large groups. Training included having the animals run in varying narrow and wide circles to strengthen their reaction to commands, and quick movement. Horses were trained to withstand noise and the smell of firearms to prevent panic on the battlefield. The most sought-after horses were those with a strong character and a natural aggressive spirit befitting situations of intense fighting. There was even a proverb saying that only a horse that kicks and bites is a good horse.

After finishing their training suitable horses were transferred to the Takeda army, which had at any time, according to the *Koyo Gunkan* chronicle, around 9000 suitable mounts (for example, in 1572 the army included 9121 mounted samurai). To these must be added the pack horses. Breeding and training a horse was not the responsibility of the individual Takeda samurai; it was done by professionals overseen by the clan's military institutions, ensuring that certain standards were met by all horses used in the army. Of course, running a system like this that kept 30% of the armed forces mounted required money which could not come from great agricultural surpluses, as the Takeda did not own much first-rate agricultural land. Instead they invested early in mining, and the gold mines of Kai were just that – gold mines. Horses were provided to a high, universal standard and then used by qualified samurai. Of course, their stipends did not need to comprise the money needed to buy, feed or train horses. The system also saved time. The daimyo could always count on basic standards being met by his mounted troops, and he could move a large part of his army faster throughout his territory, which was surrounded by potential and actual enemies in all directions who could attack any time or were to be attacked.

The Takeda breeding methods were so famous that one of Tokugawa Ieaysu's first steps after finally defeating Takeda Katsuyori in 1582 was to take the latter's horse specialists into his own service. Ironically Ieyasu had been in Oda Nobunaga's army at Nagashino seven years earlier and observed from close distance how the Takeda cavalry was stopped and decimated. However, he must have realized that it was not the horses but bad tactics deployed by the commander that caused the catastrophe. However, no other daimyo ever tried to copy the Takeda with their former mounted crack force. Mounted troops were to be one troop type among others which were no less important. Mirroring Late Medieval European developments, some samurai or rather their masters now decided to have them dismount for battle, which was observed by Frois himself in 1585. This would have been unthinkable a few generations earlier.

Once Japan had opened to the West in the mid-19th century, a trend emerged to westernize almost everything, including the military. Western-style cavalry regiments were established and a large number of horses imported. Eventually, these bigger animals supplanted Japanese horses at the breeding farms. A Japanese cavalry officer, Captain Baron Nishi, even went on to win the

Bows and Archery Equipment

1. Japanese longbows (*yumi*) made of wood, bamboo, rattan and lacquer.
1a View from the front
1b Standard arrow (*ya*)
2. Types of arrows
3. Arrowheads, from left to right: *sampaku* ("curtain-splicer"); *marune togari-y*a; *kabura-ya*, also known as *hikime-ya* (whistling arrow with holes for air intake); *karimata* variant with fork-shaped blade; *kabura-ya* adding a *karimata* blade to the whistle. Other arrow types used for signaling included flaming arrows and arrow-mounted rockets.
4. Rolled-up spare bowstring (*tsuru-maku*) made of hemp, sinew or silk.
5. Quiver (*utsubo*). This model held fewer arrows than others but offered better protection against the weather. Coat of arms: *kuwa-no mon* (melon flower), belonging to the Oda family.
6. Quiver (*shiko*): large capacity, little protection.
7. Bow and open quiver could be carried in this manner (after *Zohyo Monogatari*, c. 1657).
8. Alternative arrangement for carrying two bows including spare bowstrings (*yumidai*).
9. Bowman at the ready. *Shiko* quiver is tied to his belt at the back, arrows to be pulled with right hand.
10. Bowman covered by a *tate* pavise with *utsubo* quiver tied to his right hip.

Arquebus (*teppo*) stored on a wall rack
Main Tower of Himeji Castle

gold medal at the 1932 Olympic jumping competition riding a horse of Western descent. These days only a handful of remote areas have maintained small populations of native Japanese horses. They can be found in Hokkaido, in the Kiso Valley (an old Takeda territory), in Southern Kyushu in Kumamoto and Kagoshima, and also on the small island of Yonaguni in the deep Southwest of Okinawa Prefecture. These are the places where visitors can still see horses that resemble samurai horses, usually bay, dun or chestnut-coloured with expressive faces, long manes and tails, and with an average height of 132 cm.

Yet another aspect of the Takeda *kiba-gundan* has survived. Kamakura houses the headquarters of the Takeda Ichimon, the Takeda-style school for mounted archery (*kyuba*) under their 36th master. This is one of two still-extant schools of mounted archery in Japan, which had secretly survived under the protection of the daimyo family Hosokawa. The other school belongs to the Ogasawara family and places focus on *yabusame* ritual shooting while galloping along plain tracks in the precincts of Shinto shrines. Takeda Ichimon in contrast focuses on *kasagake* – riding and shooting on rough, broken terrain just like on a battlefield. At *kasagake* archers do not aim at targets on ground level but on targets at shoulder height. The group consists of fewer than 50 archers but they have done overseas tours.

Infantry I: Specialists with Polearms

Lance-armed troops made up the bulk of a Sengoku army. Some were mounted samurai, many more were foot soldiers, put together always more than 50% of all combatants. Until the Kamakura Period (1185–1333) almost the only forms of polearm used were the *naginata*, a "sword lance" with a long, curved blade fixed to a rather short pole and the even shorter *nagamaki*, a mixture of naginata and katana sword. During the Nambokucho Period (1333–1392) the naginata blade became smaller while the curve diminished until a straight lance with a relatively short blade emerged as the new main weapon. It was called *yari,* and its pole consisted of a core made of oak and bamboo which was lacquered as a protection against the elements. The straight blade was made of steel. Its length varied, and it could have one or two cross-blades in various patterns. On the other end of a good *yari* there was a metal cap protecting the shaft and adding punch to a two-way use.

Samurai mostly purchased and thus selected their own gear, leading to a wide array of *yari* types and lengths among them. Ashigaru (foot soldiers), however, were equipped from their lord´s arsenal, giving their armament much more uniformity. A very long lance, in fact a pike, was called *nagae-yari*. Soldiers using this weapon belonged to one of three types of specialized ashigaru weapons units. The nagae-yari´s prescribed length varied from clan to clan; Oda Nobunaga preferred a pike length of over seven metres while the Tokugawa were content with 4.5 metres (on *yari-saya*, see vol. 2) Together with the yari came a sheath to protect the blade from the elements when not in battle; before battle, this sheath was to be stored inside the ashigaru's breastplate, adding another modest layer of protection.

Ashigaru were recruited from the non-samurai classes, mainly peasants. They were organized in separate units for the three main weapons (lance, bow, and gun). The basic unit was a *kumi* (roughly a platoon), of which several formed a *ban* (a company). Terminology varied however, and some daimyo called their elite troops covering the HQ a *ban*. In major clans, many of these ashigaru were professional soldiers, well-trained, and respected as such. On the battlefield, nagae-yari units were usually drawn up in one single long line, not many ranks deep as European pikemen fought. However, the position they assumed to receive a mounted charge was similar: the nagae-yari ashigaru knelt, stuck the end of their pike into the ground and directed its raised blade at the horsemen and their mounts. The standard target of the pikes was the horses' bellies. Common doctrine recommended not to attack charging samurai first but to receive their onslaught. When engaging other nagae-yari ashigaru or other foot troops the unit moved forward in one coordinated line with their weapons held with both hands and leveled or raised. The soldiers performed perfectly synchronous, well-drilled movements with their pikes which made their unit look like a spiked wave closing in at walking speed, shaking the enemy's confidence, especially if their own lances were shorter. Coming into striking distance, the pikes were used to strike down the enemy's lances and were thrust forward and back again, either horizontally, but more often downwards from a raised position. Oda Nobunaga raised the effect of this by making his very long pikes' shafts hollow. Shafts were assembled from small pieces of bamboo and wood, then lacquered. When waved energetically, flexible pike shafts gained momentum and hit opponents even harder from above. Yari fencing in close formation required much training and unit coherence, and usually not very many ashigaru were in the elite nagae-yari units. Troops that followed up armed with shorter lances would stab at the weak points of their opponents' armour. Nagae-yari troops initially let their weapons come in from above to hit their opponents hard on their helmets or shoulders. Men thus struck became dizzy, stumbled and let their guard down, which made it possible to stab them with the same weapon. The usage of nagae-yari was different from the shorter lances preferred by samurai and described above.

Discipline was emphasized for nagae-yari units. They were not to pursue enemies over more than one *cho* (slightly over 100 metres) and had to defend units of bannermen and the lord's personal standards (*uma-jirushi*) when needed (*Zohyo Monogatari*, p. 19).

Many modern illustrations of yari fighting techniques get the position of the hands and arms wrong. The left arm/hand was used to aim at the target and the right arm/hand was used to thrust powerfully at it. Other positions included raising both arms to hold the yari overhead, with the blades pointing downwards at the target.

Besides being an effective fighting weapon in trained hands, yari could also be used to jump over small streams or walls in pole-vaulter fashion. Baggage could be carried tied to them, and even laundry could dry on yari. They were also useful when constructing a camp or measuring distances.

Infantry II: Missile Troops (Bow and Arquebus)

Until the late 12th century the Japanese longbow (*yumi*) was made of a single piece of wood but grew into a more sophisticated artifact in the following periods. While usually being six feet long, the bow core was made of wood gained from cedar, catalpa, mulberry, or the Japanese wax tree. The wooden core was covered with bamboo pieces which were glued on using fishbone or deerbone paste. Finally, the bow was lacquered (colourless, black, red, brown or multi-colour) and sometimes strengthened by winding more material tightly around it. The bow now was sturdy, flexible and powerful. It could shoot arrows up to 314.8 metres, as a test conducted in Japan in 1995 showed, but it became efficient only from about 60 metres distance. In the Edo Period samurai actually performed an experiment which saw 13.053 arrows shot within 24 hours. This means that a trained shot should have been able to release about nine arrows per minute. In the Sengoku Period the bow was not used much by samurai on the mass-battlefield but by units of specialized ashigaru fighting on foot. These not only fought skirmishes but released arrows in well-drilled formations. Once enemy troops had come close, bow-armed units were supposed to withdraw and let their own army's sword and lance-armed units do the close-order fighting. However, this did not always work, and so some bows were armed with a small bayonet-like blade, the *hazuyari*, mounted on the upper end of the bow. This turned the bow into an emergency lance of about two metres length. Bowmen were instructed to use it to strike at the faces or gaps in their opponents' armour, and later draw their swords for self-defence. As ashigaru swords were of a lower quality than samurai blades, the *Zohyo Monogatari* handbook strongly advises against striking straight at a helmet as the blade might break. Instead, attackers' arms and legs were more suitable targets for ashigaru swords.

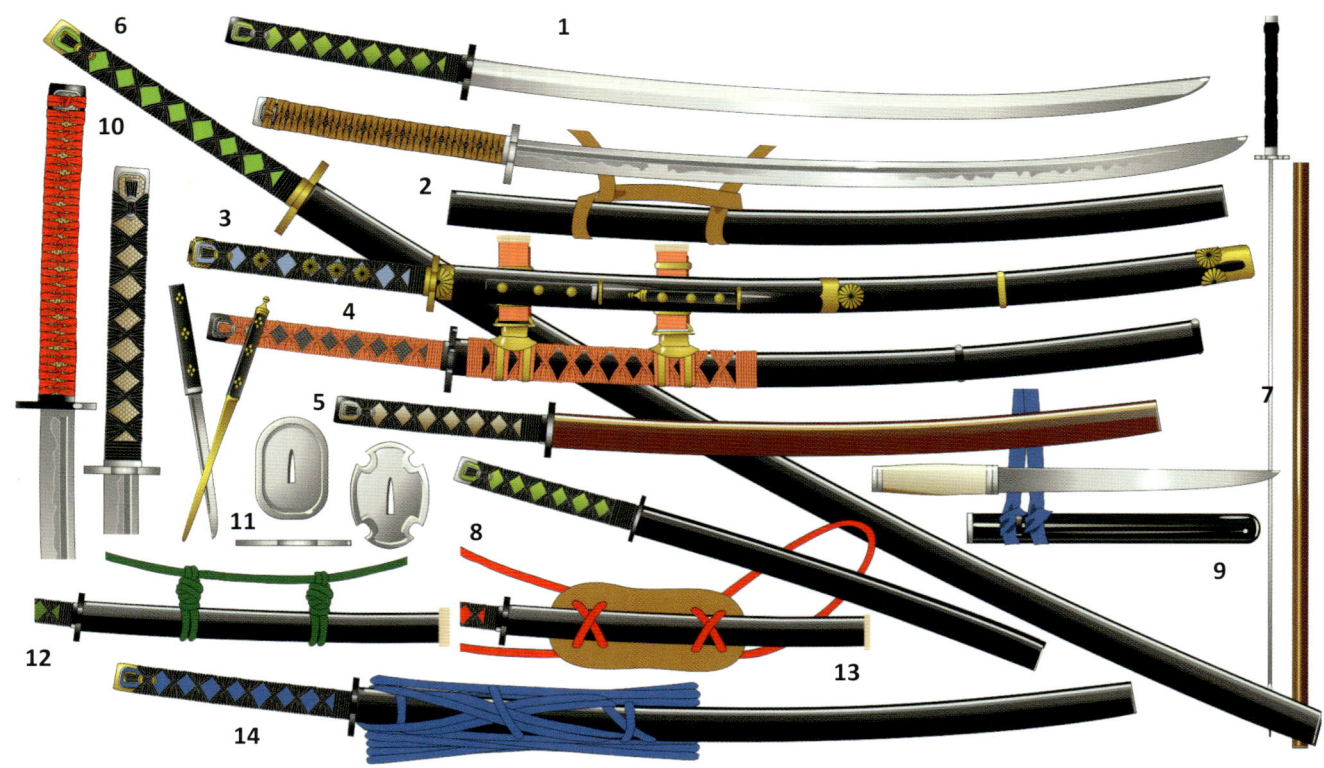

Swords and Accessories

1. *Tachi* sword. Blade without *hamon* (wavy hardening line).
2. Simply mounted *katana* and scabbard (*saya*) for *tachi*-mounting style, called a *handachi*.
3. *Tachi*
4. *Tachi*-mounted *katana* with additional cord (*ito*) wrapped around the scabbard to prevent chafing
5. Shortened *tachi* in *katana* scabbard.
6. Long (*dai*) *tachi*, blade length c. 105 cm, to be carried on a samurai´s back. A difficult to handle, but potentially very dangerous weapon.
7. Long *katana* and scabbard seen from the side
8. Short sword (*wakizashi*), blade length up to 60 cm, but often shorter.
9. *Tanto aikuchi*, a dagger without guard. Ideal for hiding inside one´s robes, often used by women.
10. Details of *ito* wrapping on the hilt. Below the cords there is another cover for which grip-enhancing ray skin was preferred. Several small metal parts such as *menuki* (ornament), *mekugi* (peg), *kogai* (sword needle), and *kozuka* (handle) are part of an assembled sword.
11. Two *kozuka* (handles), useful as small utility knives and two sturdy *tsuba* (sword guards). According to Yamamoto Kansuke (d. 1561) *tsuba* for *katana* should be about 10 cm across, which is about 20% larger than many later Edo Period *tsuba*. Tsukahara Bokuden (d. 1571) preferred an old *tsuba* over a new one even if the old one was thinner because it had seasoned over many years, and, if unbroken, protected the swordsman´s hand.

12–14. Examples for mounting a *tachi* at the left hip, still preferred by mounted samurai in the Sengoku Period while foot troops switched to katana thrust into their cloth *obi*. Tsukahara Bokuden also had advice on *obi*: the cloth belt should not be too thick as this could make drawing the sword awkward.

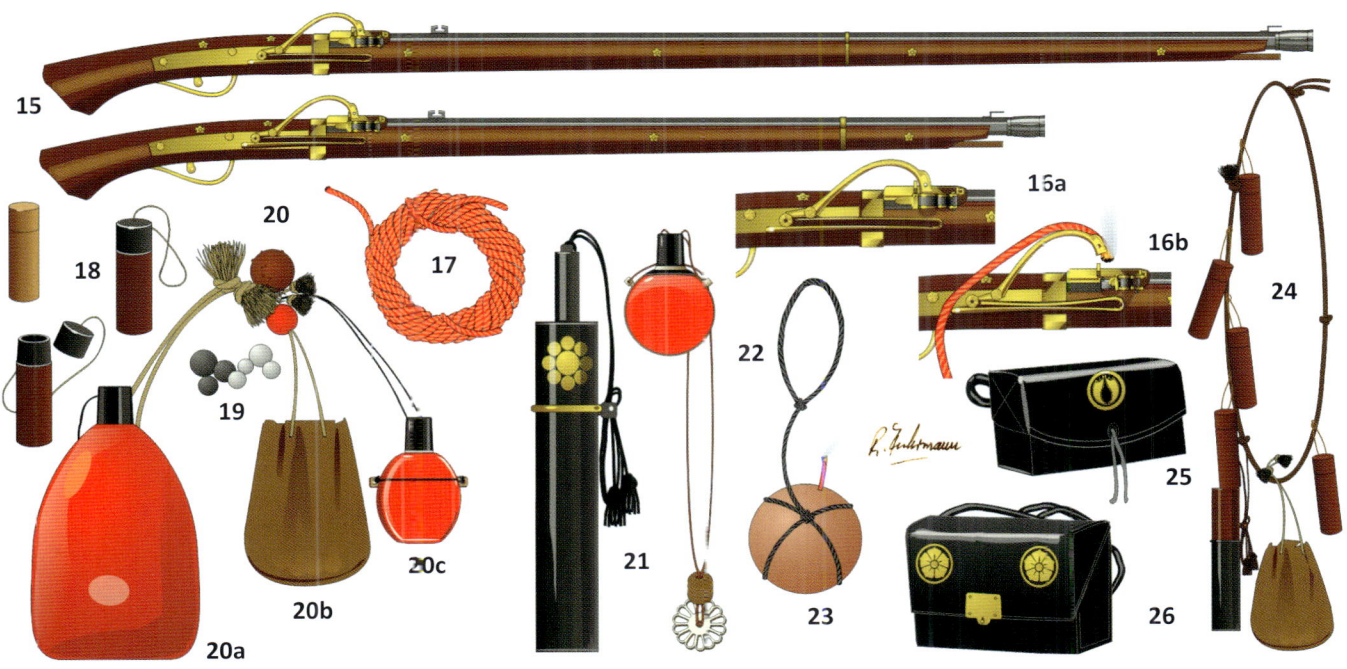

Arquebus and Accessories

- **15** Matchlock arquebus (*teppo* or *tanegashima*).
- **16a** Cock idled, sear closed.
- **16b** Cock with burning fuse, sear opened.
- **17** Fuse made of cotton. There was some variety in size and quality.
- **18** Various *hayago*, prepared charges allowing for a faster rate of fire.
- **19** Balls, mostly cast from lead, but stone and porcelain balls have also been found.
- **20** a,c: powder flasks, b: bag for balls.
- **21–22** Powder flasks protected against wetness by lacquer coating. Powder was also useful against snakebite. *Zohyo Monogatari* recommended to burn 1 *monme* (3.75g) on the bitten skin.
- **23** *Horoku*, a football-sized clay ball filled with explosives, to be thrown against fortified enemy positions or ships using the sling.
- **24** *Hayago* charges arranged in the Japanese version of the "Twelve Apostles", with ball bag and powder flasks. *Hayago* made the ko-gashira's task to resupply his gunners much easier.
- **25–26** Rectangular cases for *hayago* were more common. Made of wood with spaces for the charges, and covered with leather decorated with the daimyo's crests or badges. Small cases were carried at the right forward hip, large versions with straps on the back.

Since bow range and rate of fire were higher than that of the other main missile weapon used, the arquebus, bowmen were frequently used to cover handgunners who were reloading. Pictorial sources of battle formations sometimes show groups of five or more gunners with a similar number of archers close by. In other cases, units of five are mixed such as two, three or four gunners with three, two or one archer. In the middle of the Edo Period the Matsuura fielded three archers for every ten arquebusiers, but in the preceding Sengoku Period the number of archers was higher than that. The Takeda had two archers for three arquebusiers in the 1560´s. Other less potent and especially earlier daimyo had more archers than handgunners.

The matchlock arquebus, called *teppo* or *tanegashima*, had, theoretically, a wider range of about 500 metres but there was little hope of accurately hitting and damaging anything that was more than 50 metres away. However, once the target had closed in to 20 metres it was devastating, usually piercing all traditional forms of armour. The further the teppo spread since arriving in 1542/43, the more pressing this problem became; and evidence shows that many of the victims were high-ranking samurai in the frontline of attack. The answer to the new challenge was the introduction of "modern" armour (*tosei gusoku*) which often sported massive breastplates in Western style. Some of these survive today with visible dents in the front plates. These came from deliberately firing of arquebuses at them to demonstrate that the armour was bullet-proof.

Apart from its short effective range the teppo´s other disadvantages were its low rate of fire (three to four shots a minute, compared to nine for the bow) and its vulnerability to the effects of rain and humidity. However, as a mixed-arms unit bowmen and arquebusiers could counterbalance their respective weaknesses. As an added bonus, it took much less time to train a farmer´s son-turned-ashigaru as a teppo gunner than as an archer, and less physical strength than needed to become a nagae-yari fighter.

The other name for the arquebus, *tanegashima*, points to the island in Kyushu where shipwrecked Portuguese first introduced it to Japan. Technologically, this weapon was not as close to European battlefield arms as to its Southeast Asian offspring mostly used for hunting which was lighter and more adaptable to Japan´s mobile style of warfare. Japan´s arms makers were quickly able to produce teppo with suitable alterations. In 1544 the new weapon came to the attention of the religious fighters of the Negoro temple on the Kii Peninsula, not very far from the capital, Kyoto. The teppo also drew interest from the merchants and craftsmen of Sakai, close to today´s City of Osaka. In 1545 shogun Ashikaga Yoshiharu witnessed a teppo demonstration in Kyoto. This came as a signal to ambitious daimyo across Japan to order and buy up ever greater numbers of teppo. Western and Central Japan were in a more advantageous position to obtain quantities of teppo. Besides the rush for the new hardware there were problems obtaining sufficient quantities and qualities of sulphur to make black powder. Japan only had a limited ability to produce sulphur, and furthermore the shogun and a small number of daimyo kept the recipe secret. Thus it was possible only for a select number of daimyo to quickly build large squads of gunners and use the new weapon effectively to quash their rivals in Sengoku Japan.

Samurai did not consider the new weapon as something not be fitting their status or even a coward´s weapon as it was claimed in 1979 by Noel Perrin in his otherwise thought-provoking book "Giving Up the Gun: Japan's Reversion to the Sword, 1543–1879". On the contrary, many samurai owned a gun. When ownership was restricted at the turn of the 16th and 17th centuries this happened because it was considered as destabilizing the social order since it gave power to the lower classes. Samurai, however, were not barred from owning a gun.

There were various calibers of teppo. Ashigaru units usually had guns with smaller calibers of 1 or 2 *monme*. 1 *monme* means a caliber of 8.5 mm. Larger guns had a caliber of up to 100 monme (= 48 mm!), but these giant teppo were very heavy and difficult to operate, which meant they were most frequently used in static warfare such as sieges (see volume 2).

Units armed with bows or guns (*yumi-tai* and *teppo-tai*) usually comprised 25, 30, 50 or more men led by an officer called *ashigaru-daisho*. Another officer with the rank of *bugyo* was responsible for the special weapons and for training with them. Below these men came *yoriki* (junior officers), *kashira* ("sergeants") and *ko-gashira* ("corporals"). Usually there was one ko-gashira for every five men. Besides these men in the front lines, a number of men was needed to bring up ammunition supplies for bows and guns, usually carried in large wooden boxes.

Besides commanding their men, ko-gashira had several other functions to perform. They were expected to pre-determine the right distance for shooting. For this they carried a stick which doubled as their symbol of authority. A ko-gashira of archers carried a supply of arrows which he handed to his men. These first used up the arrows supplied to them in this way, then turned to the supply they themselves carried in quivers. Each ko-gashira was resupplied by a man carrying more arrows in bundles or boxes of 100 or 200. Therefore, the basic unit of archers consisted of seven men, of which five actually fired arrows.

A ko-gashira of teppo arquebusiers would similarly supply his men from a box next to him. Gunners usually wrapped their burning fuses around their lower arms, but they had a tendency to burn out. In that case the ko-gashira stepped in and supplied a new burning fuse from several he had wrapped around his own lower left arm. If that was not sufficient, there were small metal holders for burning fuses to be planted firmly into the ground close to the ko-gashira.

Conch trumpet blower at Ishida Mitsunari´s HQ, 1600
Sekigahara Reenactment, 2000

Honjin – The Headquarters Unit

With the army in position, its commander-in-chief *(sodaisho)* sat down on his folding camp stool in the middle or towards the rear of his troops, preferably slightly elevated with a good view of everything. The commander´s coolness and visible confidence were important to his men, so utter calmness was asked for in his demeanor. He was assisted by several valets *(kosho)*, samurai boys still in training who had not yet undergone their *genpuku* (coming of age) ceremony. Their status as adolescents was symbolized by their unshaven forelocks. Oda Nobunaga´s favourite valet, Mori Ranmaru (b. 1565), shot to fame when he died a fighting death together with his lord in 1582.

Other personnel surrounding the commander in his *honjin* (headquarters) included senior samurai, staff officers, personal retainers, messengers, standard bearers, signallers, support troops and porters, doctors, specialists for washing and grooming head trophies, sometimes even priests, and certainly elite troops serving in lifeguard units. The latter had great responsibility because a dead commander usually meant defeat in battle. The fact that Uesugi Kenshin was able to get physically close to his rival Takeda Shingen at Kawanakajima in 1561 clearly shows the desperate situation of the Takeda that had forced them to send headquarters troops into battle earlier on. Typically, mounted samurai were the most senior of these elite troops. Oda Nobunaga even had two units of *umawari-shu* (mounted lifeguards), one distinguished by wearing a black, the other a red *horo,* which was a huge cloak worn on a bamboo and wicker frame on the back of a samurai´s armour. Toyotomi Hideyoshi surpassed this by having his lifeguards wear an even larger gold *horo*. Concerning numbers, Hojo Ujiyasu had 94 mounted samurai in this unit in 1559, later 120, each with a groom on foot *(kinju)*. The primary roles of these elite mounted samurai were scouting, escorting, and as a reserve strike force in battle. Other HQ troops could be selected groups of foot samurai and ashigaru with long lances, guns or bows, very often with uniform armour of superior quality and back flags identical within one unit. Basically, HQ troops provide an overview of an entire clan army *en miniature* complete with various troop types.

Staff officers included the chief of staff *(gunshi, gunbugyo)* and various advisers *(gunshi, gunkan,* or *gunsha)*. The important job of battlefield analyst and provost was performed by the *o-metsuke* who doubled as the commander of *ikusa-metsuke* and observed and reported the performances of all units and individuals.

Another distinguished group stationed at HQ were the *tsukai-ban* or mounted messengers. Many difficult and dangerous tasks were given to them. Performing well required courage, superior riding skills, an ability to understand and judge fast, and even sufficiently polite manners which were needed to communicate with samurai holding much higher rank. Tsukai-ban samurai were chosen by the lord from his direct retainers owing complete obedience to him. They were sent out during battle to relay the commander's urgent wishes and to relay important information. As it was important to have everybody recognize their own tsukai-ban from afar (so as not to lose them owing to "friendly fire"), they wore very distinctive back flags like the famous centipede sashimono of the Takeda tsukai-ban, and often colourful horo (see figure on p. 103). The elite status of the tsukai-ban was further enhanced by their small number: just 29 for the large army of Toyotomi Hideyoshi, and 40 for the biggest Sengoku army belonging to Tokugawa Ieyasu. There was also a second group of military messengers, runners on foot whose status did not come close to the mounted tsukai-ban.

Some elite samurai including umawari-shu and tsukai-ban were marked by a horo cloak, sometimes in addition to another form of sashimono. A horo was a sack-like shape tailored from colourful silk or cloth, fixed to a light bamboo or wicker, basket-like frame. When riding, the wind blew through this structure and made its colours, patterns or dyed or sewed on crests highly visible. Seen from the front, as soldiers that came under attack would perceive them, the horo almost doubled the size of an attacking mounted samurai and must have looked intimidating. There is also the opinion that a horo protected a samurai's back against arrows, but this is a controversial claim. However, it made messengers stand out from a long distance.

Another key element of a honjin were ashigaru acting as signallers. Some used bells (*kane*), gongs (*dora*) or wooden clappers (*hyoshigi* which can still be heard at Kabuki theatrical performances today). Certainly, all field armies used drums of various sizes and conch trumpets (*horagai* or simply *kai*). Big drums that had to be transported on carts were called *taiko* which often required a three-man-crew to operate. Drums were an important part of the soundtrack to everyday military life: They were beaten to mark every sixth step on the march, transmitted orders or the time when the army was in camp, and were used to encourage soldiers in battle.

Blowing the *horagai* conch trumpet was a time-honoured means of military communication in Japan. Its moaning sound carried for miles. It was constructed by adding a metal or ceramic mouthpiece to a large conch shell which was then covered in a net with attractively dyed tassels which made handling easier. Horagai were blown for general encouragement as well as for the transmission of general orders including at night time. Members of an army had to remember the various sets of blasts.

(Next pages)
Outpost overlooking the Inland Sea manned by Chosokabe Troops, Shikoku 1585

This outpost is a typical rough field fortification that takes advantage of whatever terrain features and building resources are locally available. It is based on a pictorial scroll in the British Museum, London. Local workers have just finished building it, although the samurai in charge of this area does not seem too happy with the job they have done. Will this stand up to the might of Toyotomi Hideyoshi's invasion army? Certainly there will be enough food supplies as these are just being brought up by ashigaru.

The unsophisticated construction and the lack of uniformity among the troops emphazise the slightly backward character of military development in Shikoku. However, cleverly using trees and the nature of terrain for protection is an ancient samurai art. The seaward side is well protected by a cliff and a stake palisade. Small platforms covered by lengths of cloth with the Chosokabe *mon* dyed or painted on offer some protection from the elements. There is a fighting platform on top of the wooden gate, which has been blocked by a mobile wall of *tate* pavises.

In 1585, firmly in control of most of Honshu, Toyotomi Hideyoshi sent 90,000 men in 700 ships to conquer Shikoku, which had just been unified by the daimyo of Tosa, Chosokabe Motochika (1538-1599). Shikoku was off the mainstream of contemporary military modernisation, and the Chosokabe relied on an archaic system in which most foot soldiers were still real peasants working the fields, only being called up for campaigns. Obtaining more standardized equipment and training was difficult, and most military units in Shikoku were rather militias than parts of a standing army. Chosokabe Motochika put up enough resistance (defense of Ichinomiya Castle) to save face but entered negotiations fast enough to secure Hideyoshi's pardon. The Chosokabe lost possession of those parts of Shikoku they had recently conquered but remained daimyo of Tosa. Motochika became a faithful vassal of Hideyoshi and joined his campaigns against Odawara and Korea in 1590 and 1592.

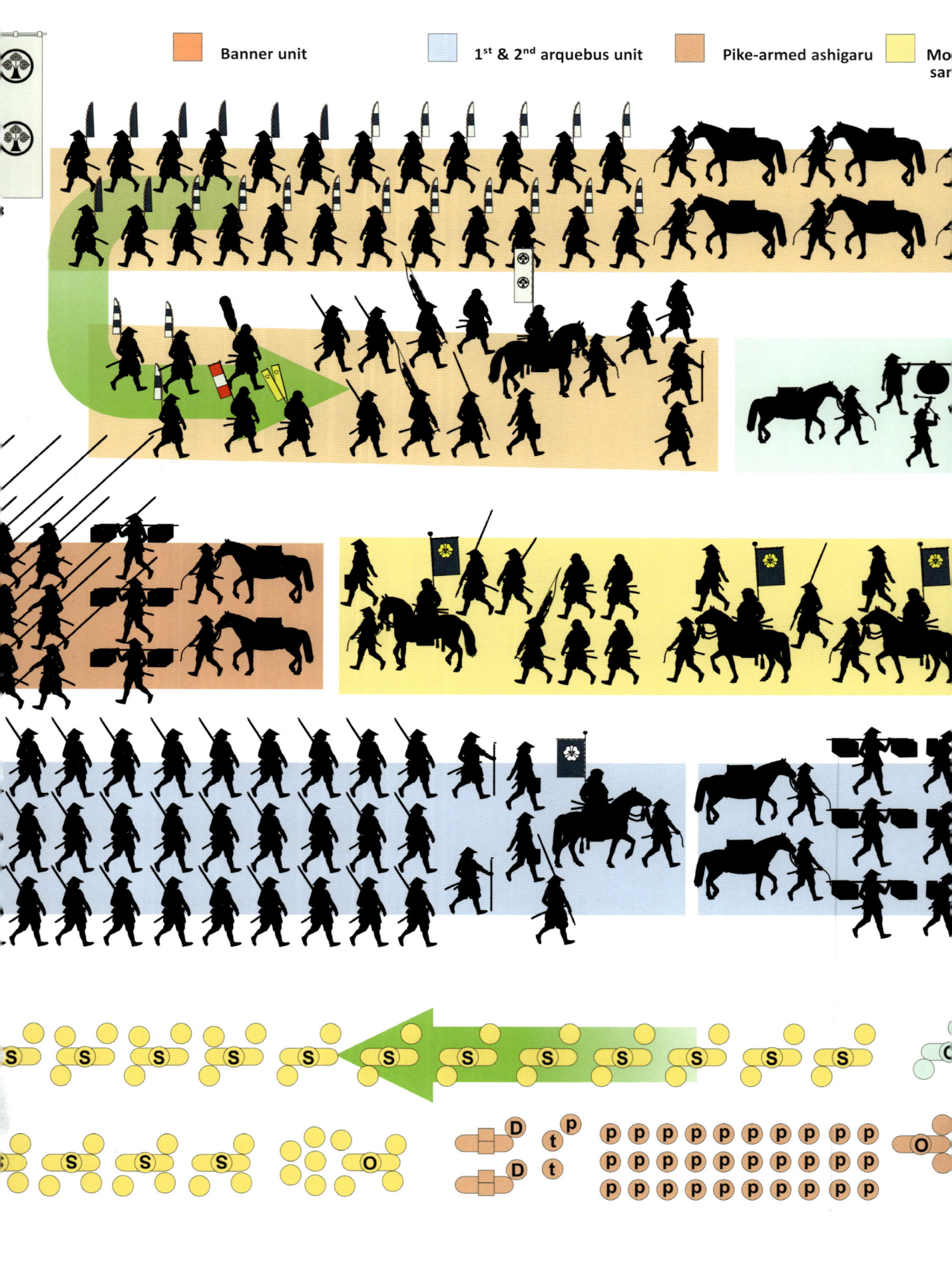

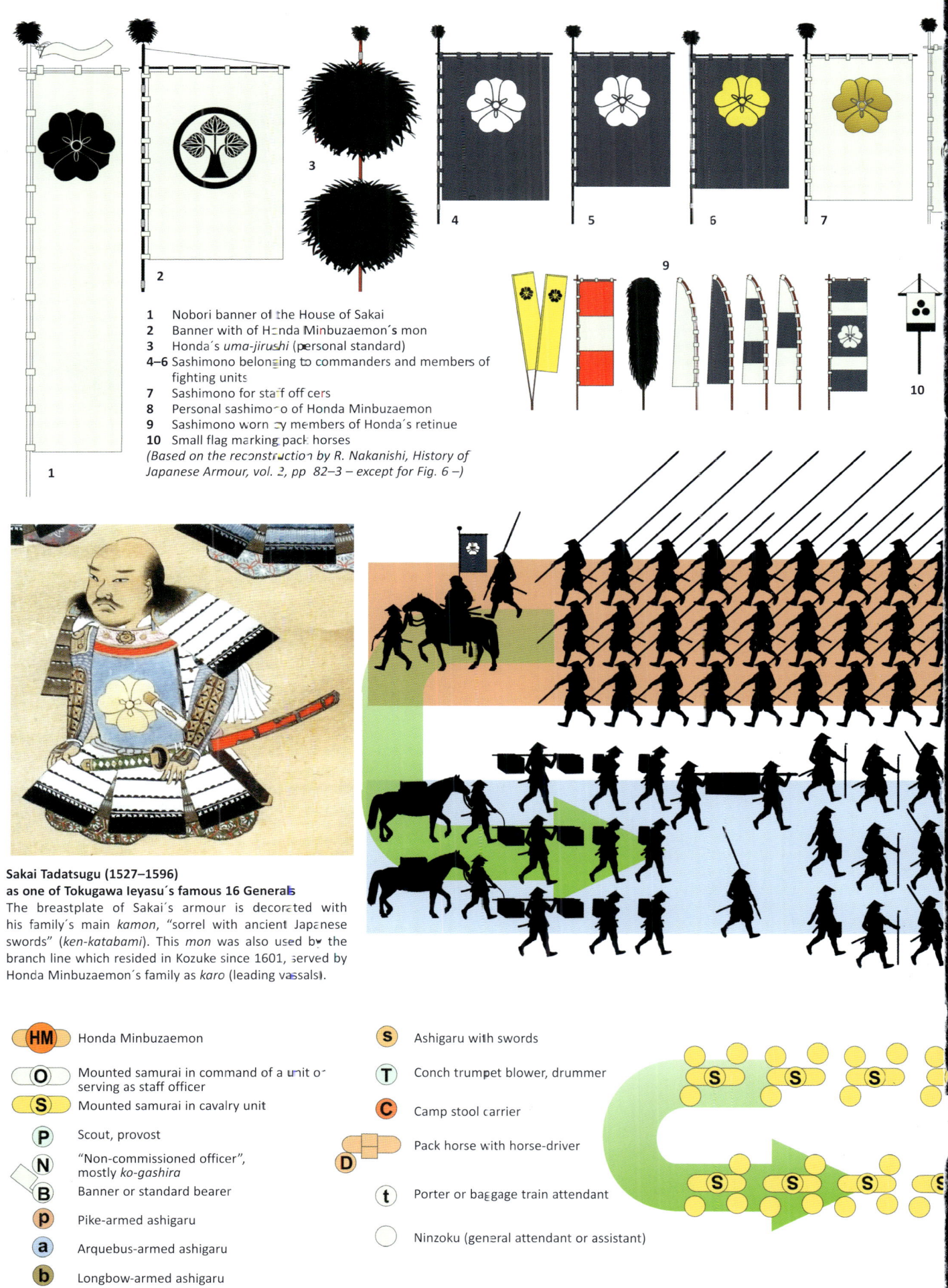

1 Nobori banner of the House of Sakai
2 Banner with of Honda Minbuzaemon's mon
3 Honda's *uma-jirushi* (personal standard)
4–6 Sashimono belonging to commanders and members of fighting units
7 Sashimono for staff officers
8 Personal sashimono of Honda Minbuzaemon
9 Sashimono worn by members of Honda's retinue
10 Small flag marking pack horses
(Based on the reconstruction by R. Nakanishi, History of Japanese Armour, vol. 2, pp 82–3 – except for Fig. 6 –)

Sakai Tadatsugu (1527–1596)
as one of Tokugawa Ieyasu's famous 16 Generals
The breastplate of Sakai's armour is decorated with his family's main *kamon*, "sorrel with ancient Japanese swords" (*ken-katabami*). This *mon* was also used by the branch line which resided in Kozuke since 1601, served by Honda Minbuzaemon's family as *karo* (leading vassals).

- **HM** Honda Minbuzaemon
- **O** Mounted samurai in command of a unit or serving as staff officer
- **S** Mounted samurai in cavalry unit
- **P** Scout, provost
- **N** "Non-commissioned officer", mostly *ko-gashira*
- **B** Banner or standard bearer
- **p** Pike-armed ashigaru
- **a** Arquebus-armed ashigaru
- **b** Longbow-armed ashigaru
- **s** Ashigaru with swords
- **T** Conch trumpet blower, drummer
- **C** Camp stool carrier
- **D** Pack horse with horse-driver
- **t** Porter or baggage train attendant
- ○ Ninzoku (general attendant or assistant)

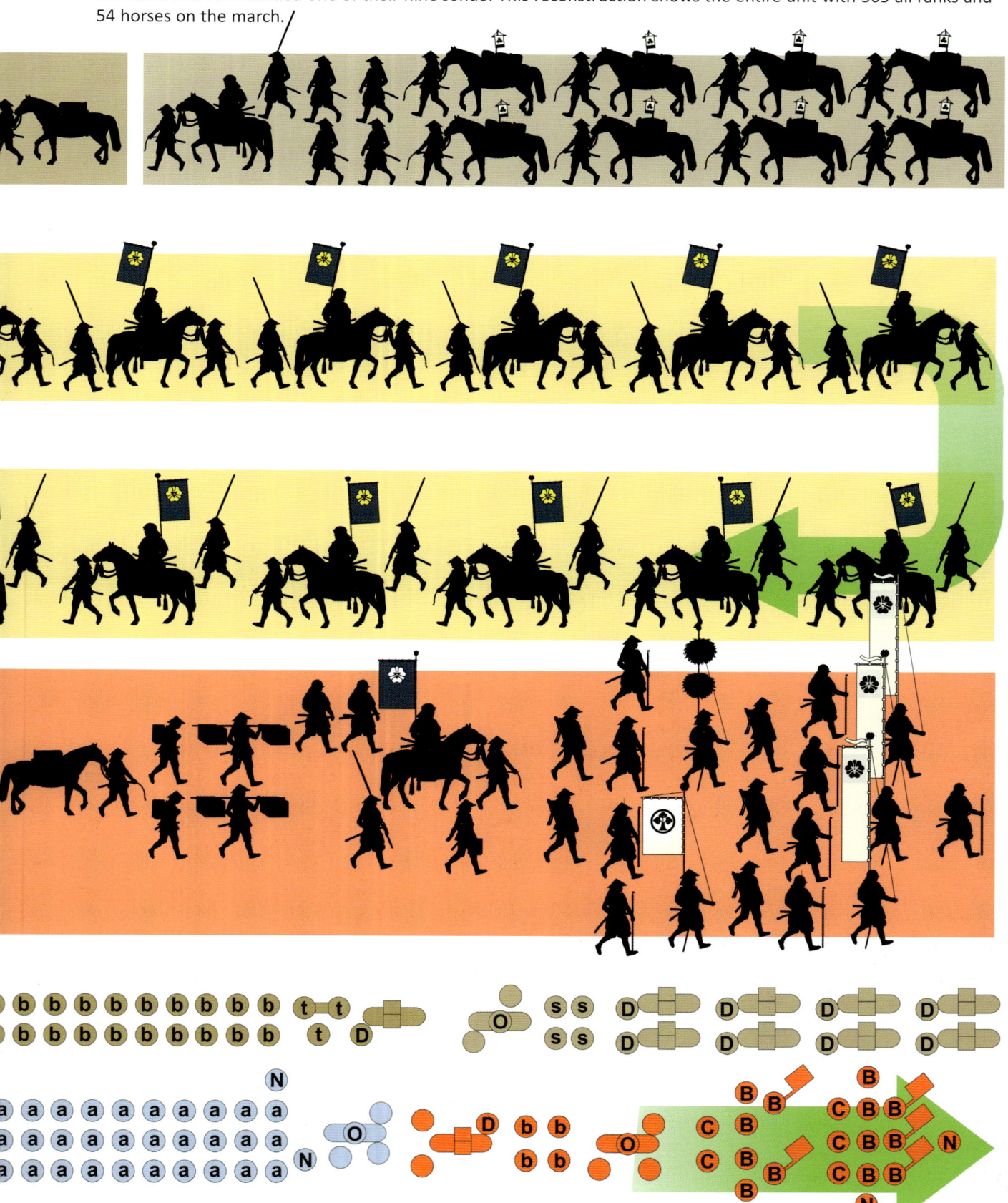

Sakai Military Unit under Honda Minbuzaemon on the March

A *sonae* (unit) of the Sakai daimyo's clan army on the march. Honda Minbuzaemon was a *karo* (leading vassal) of the Sakai and commanded one of their nine *sonae*. This reconstruction shows the entire unit with 365 all ranks and 54 horses on the march.

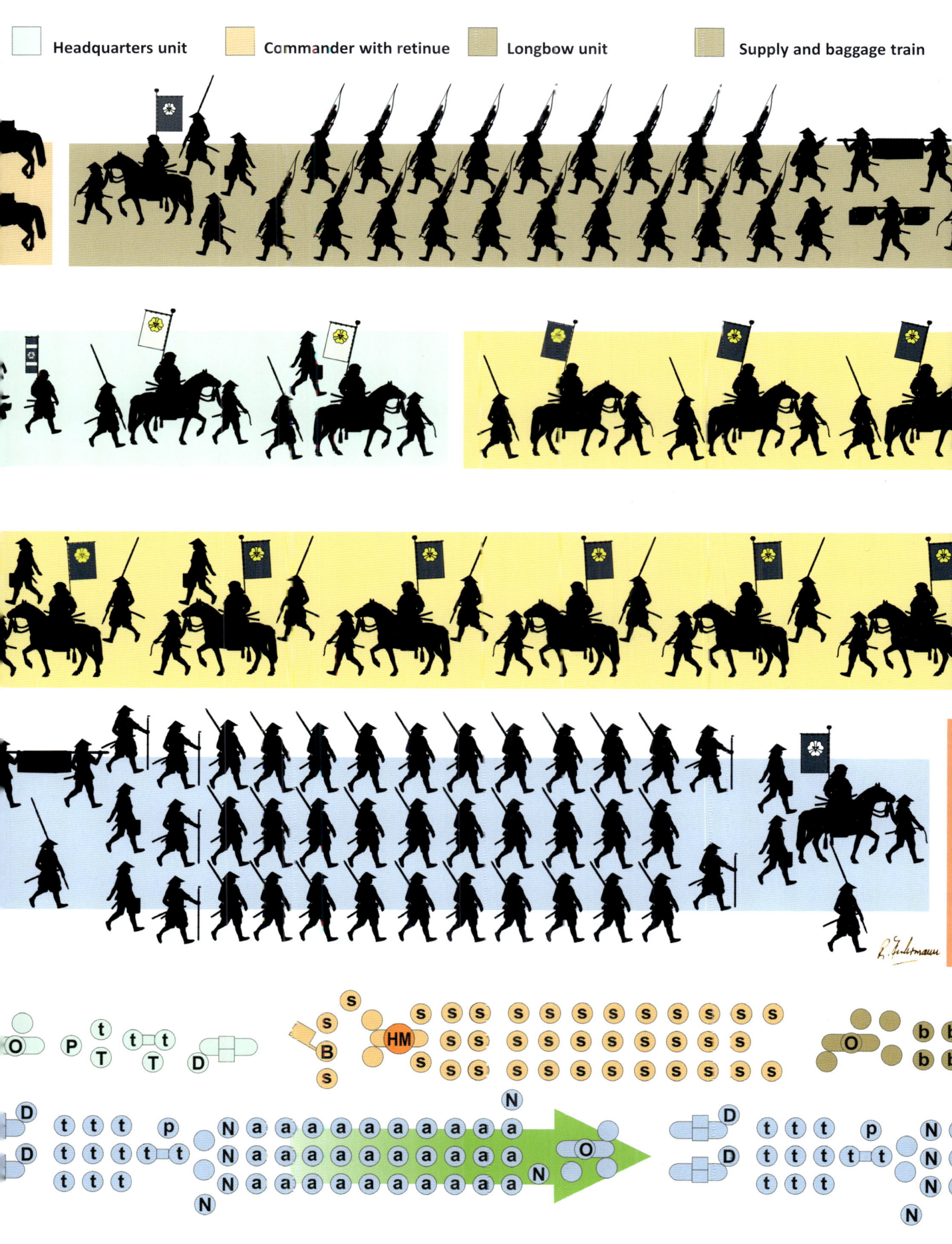

Conch trumpet (*kai, horagai*)
Takeda Shrine, Kofu, Yamanashi Pref.

Examples for Conch Trumpet Signals

Signal	Meaning
Three signals to prepare an encamped army for marching: 1st signal: 3 blasts 2nd signal: 9 blasts 3rd signal: 27 blasts.	1st signal: Finish Meal 2nd signal: Ready to march out 3rd signal: March out.
Two sets of 4 blasts; used three times during the night.	Time announced at 23.00, 1.00 and 3.00 hours.
5 blasts, to be repeated nine times.	Calling allies to battle.
Nine times 3 blasts.	Advance to pursue the enemy.

Samurai commanders knew how important communication in battle was and certainly surpassed contemporary Europeans in this respect. Besides messengers and acoustic instruments, they could also rely on "whistling arrows" which had been used by samurai for a long time. These arrows had a relatively large wooden shape with holes at the tip through which the winds whistled. There were also means to transmit signals visually such as signal rockets, usually reserved to signal important or very urgent general orders such as "Commence hostilities". In addition, smoke-signals were generated by burning different materials in large cauldrons.

The various military flags *(gunhata)* in operation were of prime importance to Sengoku armies. These also required a lot of manpower. Personal standards *(umajirushi)* and individual banners heralded a commander's presence on the battlefield, encouraged the troops and provided orientation during a melee (a more detailed treatment of all types of standards is included in volume 2). Much more numerous were large rectangular banners (*nobori no hata*) which were not given to units as their "company" or "regimental" colours but concentrated in special units of flag bearers. Fighting units were instead marked by their members' identical sashimono carried on their armoured backs, and/or ai-jirushi marks painted on their armour and jingasa helmets.

Banner units were led by their own officers. Commanding officers used them to signal to their troops. The depiction of two complete units *(sonae)* from the Takeda army in 1561 preserved in the Iwakuni Art Museum mentioned above shows the unit under Yamagata Masakage in the first battle line, followed by Takeda Shingen's own HQ unit. Yamagata has placed one long row of 15 bearers of rectangular nobori banners, decorated with five black and and five black and white bars, behind himself at the rear of his unit. Using these men he was able to signal further to the rear to his lord in his HQ. Shingen's own HQ unit includes as many as 30 such banners (in white with black Takeda *mon*). However, we see these in the centre of the formation just in front of the commander, drawn up like a cross which is missing its rear tip. With this arrangement it was possible for Shingen to signal to the front as well as to both flanks. He did not need banners at the rear because there was no other battle line behind his unit. Signals were transmitted through synchronized movements of the banners in one row, e.g. by raising and lowering them or waiving them in a predetermined pattern.

Everything in the army related to flags and banners including protection for the lord's important personal standards could come under the command of a samurai in the prestigious post of *hata-daisho*, or as a lower rank to a *hata-bugyo* or a *nobori-bugyo*.

Finally, a lord could order his men to use their voices to raise a battle-cry. This was usually used as encouragement to samurai, like the famous "Ei! Ei! Oh!" shout before the start of a battle.

Field drum (taiko)
Matsuura Museum in Hirado,
Nagasaki Pref.
This drum was carried by one man on his back and beaten by another.

Mon belonging to the Chosokabe daimyo family
The Chosokabe crest displays "sevenfold sorrel" in a ring *(nanatsu katabami)*. This motive is very rare among Japanese mon.

Utilizing this large variety of communication techniques to their full potential enabled, for instance, Uesugi Kenshin to effectively lead an army of 30, 000 at night and beat an even stronger army in a battle that was fought across a river (Tedorigawa 1577 against elements of the Oda army). Even when thick fog limited visibility drastically during the decisive battle of Sekigahara in 1600, Tokugawa Ieyasu never lost his ability to command his army. Famously, he even had guns fired at the position of a turncoat hesitating to join him. These abilities become even more striking when contrasted to the confusion at the foggy battle of Lützen in the Thirty Years War that saw King Gustav Adolphus of Sweden separated from his own men and cut down by the enemy. Tokugawa Ieyasu would never have mounted his horse to lead a charge, and he certainly made sure that there were always several hundred men of his own guards between himself and the enemy.

Supply and Baggage Train

As opposed to contemporary Europe, Sengoku commanders were keenly aware of how important effective supply units were to the overall success of the army. Consequently this branch of service, usually called *konida*, was not partly privatized and mixed up with the families of soldiers or even prostitutes and other dubious campfollowers, but organized on strictly military lines even though civilian personnel formed more than half the strength of these units. It was especially the Sengoku Period during which all aspects of military logistics became increasingly thoroughly organized, simply out of necessity because ever increasing troop numbers needed to be kept in the field during prolonged campaigns.

Ammunition for bows and teppo guns was usually carried close to the respective units which therefore could be quickly resupplied. Items belonging to individual samurai were carried by their own personal retainers and their pack horses. Other necessities however were the responsibility of the two branches of the supply train, the *onida* ("large baggage") and *konida* ("small baggage"). The "large baggage" comprised items needed for building a camp, pavises *(tate)*, and spare arms. "Small baggage" included food for men (mainly rice) and animal fodder as well as stocks of alcoholic drink *(sake* – rice wine – or *shochu*, any type of strong, distilled liquor).

If possible, heavier items were transported on two-wheeled carts drawn by oxen or supply train attendants, whereas smaller baggage travelled on pack horses. Both carts and horses often had small flags attached to them to show to whom they belonged (see illustrations on p. 79). Most baggage train attendants *(ninzoku* or *komono)* and horse drivers *(kuchitori)* were hired directly from the rural population. They wore peasants´ practical work dress, and often a knife or a short sword for self-protection. In the case of an attack, such personnel were not spared. Also included in the konida unit were a number of regular troops such as fully armed ashigaru or even samurai tasked with providing protection. In the example given below the ratio of non-military staff and armed ashigaru escorts is 10:4. It was noted that commanders were well-advised to select intelligent individuals for the escort role as situations might arise that demanded taking emergency decisions fast and independently. A quartermaster *(nizairyo)* in *Zohyo Monogatari* tells his men to never let their guard down because in enemy territory even "your allies... may rob you of your food." (p. 39).

The commander of the supply train unit held staff rank *(konida-bugyo)*, which emphasizes how vital this branch of the army was regarded. This logistics officer often headed his column on the march, at other times he worked at headquarters. Some very famous generals had been commanders of supply units in the earlier stages of their careers, among them Naito Masatoyo, one of Takeda Shingen´s famed 24 Generals, and Tokugawa Ieyasu himself.

SAMURAI AS MERCENARIES

One of the results of internal fighting in Japan during the Sengoku and early Edo Periods was a steady stream of samurai who were dispossessed because they had fought on a losing side. They became *ronin*, samurai without masters (and incomes). Among the options available was seeking opportunities abroad. Some samurai but also members of other classes became associated with the *wako*, pirates mainly operating around the Chinese coast, whereas the Spanish Philippines attracted a large number of Christian refugee samurai, among them Nobunaga´s famous general and daimyo, Takayama Ukon, who died in Manila in 1615.

Ayutthaya, capital of Siam (today´s Thailand), welcomed talented people from abroad with open arms. There were Chinese, Malaysians, Portuguese, Dutch, Indians, Persians and Japanese, who during the 16th c. were allowed to settle in a self-governed Japanese town (Nihonmachi) close to the Royal city. Many Japanese engaged in commerce, and some of the community´s leaders owned ships, which took Siamese goods to Japan (hides for manufacturing military goods were prominent among exports), and Japanese-manufactured goods, including swords, armour and firearms, to Ayutthaya. However, there was one obligation the Japanese had to fulfil to continue enjoying Royal patronage: military service.

Siamese armies were frequently fielded against their arch-enemy, Burma, as well as other regional powers. They consisted of large numbers of under-equipped, conscripted peasants and a relatively small nucleus of Royal retainers from the capital: Siamese guards, war elephants

Royal guard troops in the Kingdom of Siam.

Japanese are clearly shown in richly decorated kimono with obi belts, carrying Chinese-style ceremonial polearms and a large *hinomaru* banner. This is basically the only contemporary picture of Japanese in the service of Siam, but unfortunately an overzealous Japanese historian of the 1930´s might have worked "creatively" with the evidence, leaving a large question mark as to whether the red sun flag was actually used in Siam.

Yamada Nagamasa´s flag on one of his ships as painted on a votive tablet from the Sengen Shrine in Shizuoka.

In 1626, Yamada Nagamasa donated a large painting of the ship to his hometown shrine. This was lost in a fire in 1788, but it had been copied before and has been again many times since.

Japanese in the service of the King of Siam fighting Burmese war elephants and escorts

Drawings by Sascha Lunyakov, arranged by Thomas Körner (also released as 30mm flat zinnfiguren by WEKO/Thomas Körner)

with their handlers and foreign contingents. For several decades before and after 1600, the Japanese typically seemed to have sent about 500, sometimes 600 or 800, crack troops that were even employed as Royal palace guards at some point. Apparently, it was not difficult to find young men with fighting abilities in Nihonmachi who were willing to serve for a time. There was no pay but there was the prospect of rich booty to be made as well as adventures in exotic lands. If not needed by King's army, the Japanese returned to their usual jobs in trade, which could be conducted in a very robust way, or they manufactured goods, or fought elsewhere.

During the Siamese-Burmese battles of this age, most famously at the "Battle of the Elephants" at Nong Sarai in 1593, the Japanese also faced war elephants. Elephant warfare in Southeast Asia involved hundreds of animals crewed by warriors of high status riding them, using weapons from a huge arsenal handed to them by their assistants on the howdahs. The driver sat behind the howdah in the rear. Elephants also had a contingent of foot soldiers surrounding them, keeping enemy foot soldiers away from their master and his mount.

The Japanese fighters enjoyed a fearsome reputation and must have done well against elephants, attacking crews aggressively. They had access to the finest swords in the region and also to Japanese armour through their own trade activities. As most Southeast Asian warriors wore little armour and even few clothes, an armoured samurai with his weapons must have appeared to them like a demon from hell.

Yamada Nagamasa's mercenaries, as visualized by an early 20th c. Japanese postcard illustrator. Everybody is in his own armour, mostly haramaki type, with weapons of individual choice. Leaving out some pieces of armour and wearing light clothing is very suitable to Southeast Asia's hot climate (www.ehagaki.org).

The most famous leader of Japanese fighters in Siam was Yamada Nagamasa (c. 1590–1630), who once served as a palanquin bearer to a minor daimyo. He had received basic military training akin to that of an ashigaru. As the Sengoku Period with it its ample opportunities even for low-born people came to an end, Yamada was attracted to Ayutthaya. There he had a brilliant career both as chief of Nihonmachi, running his own specially designed ships between Siam and Japan, and as a trusted commander of the King's Japanese guards. Yamada was very status-conscious; he had his own coat of arms and banners and made sure he and his men were well armoured and armed. His downfall and end by poisoning came when the Japanese became too involved in Court intrigue. The new King turned against Nihonmachi, but later Japanese adventurers returned. However, Japan's closure of its ports to all foreigners around 1640 was such a severe blow that it terminated lucrative overseas trade and eventually meant that the steady flow of Japanese immigrants ceased. Nihonmachi faded away into history and with it the memory of the samurai fighting against war elephants.

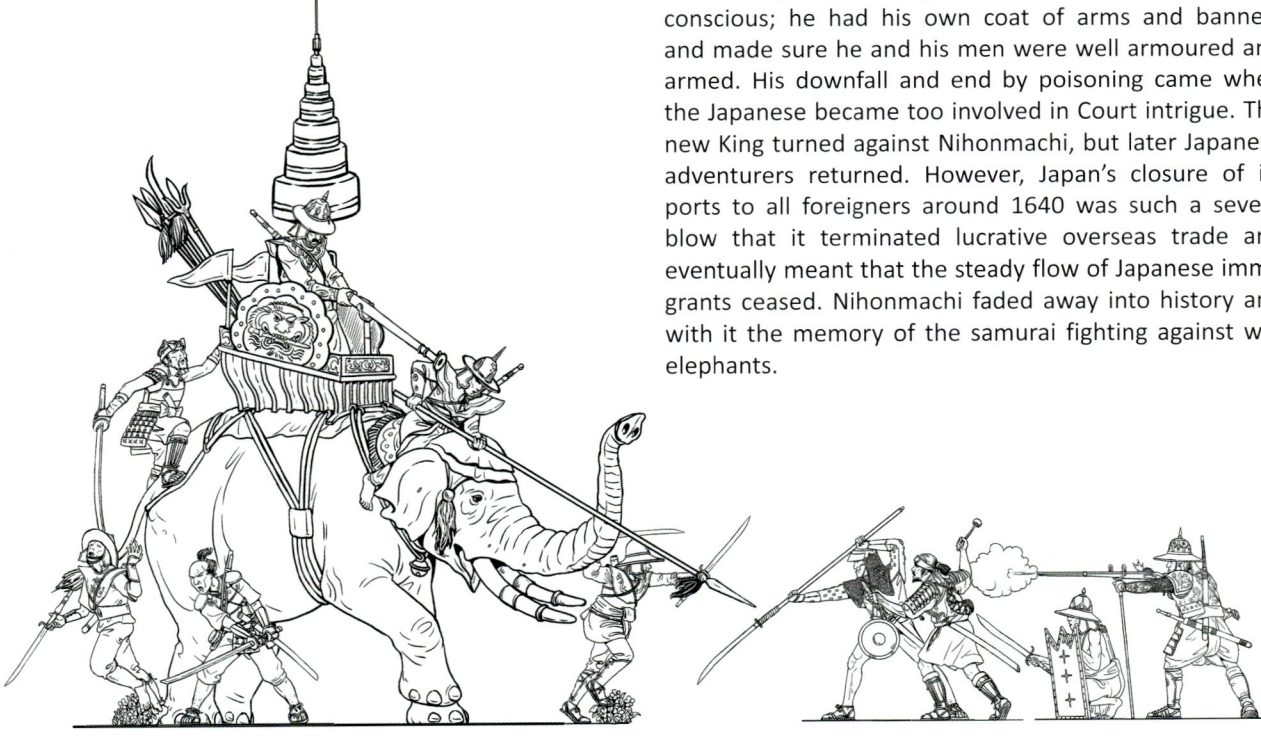

A SAMURAI ARMY IN ACTION

On the March

To study a formal military march performed by samurai, we need to turn our attention to the *sankin kotai* system, which was in force throughout most of the Edo Period following the Sengoku Period. *Sankin kotai* meant that more than 200 daimyo were required to reside in the shogun's capital, Edo (today's Tokyo) every other year, which meant that every year they were either forced to march across Japan to Edo accompanied by a large number of their troops, or to return to their fiefdoms. Protocol rules had to be keenly observed during these marches not least because breaches of protocol had to be desperately avoided. Handbooks and manuals were produced that documented these ceremonial troop movements with minute detail. In contrast, documentation about marches in the Sengoku Period is much, much scarcer. Samurai until the early 17th century had better things to do than to observe petty bureaucratic rules and draw large charts documenting routine proceedings. Fortunately, these sources from the Edo Period help us to come to solid conclusions about the preceding period.

Putting an army on the march in Japan did not only have practical purposes such as moving troops from A to B but was also designed to demonstrate status. Observing social ranks and proper procedure was also important among military men of the Sengoku Period, and a good show of military strength now and then showed the general population who was in charge. If there was time to plan the march carefully, the army was divided into a vanguard (*zengun*), a main force (*chugun*, including the headquarters), a rearguard (*kogun*) as well as the supply and baggage train (*konida*). There could also be separate units guarding the flanks of the HQ or serving as flexible detachments. If there was no time for such arrangements, e. g. in 1582 and 1583 when Toyotomi Hideyoshi's army hurried with lightning speed to Yamazaki and to Shizugatake to inflict utter surprise and defeat upon the enemy, things were handled more pragmatically. On such forced marches, the commander and his staff were in the van, followed by the fastest elements of the army: mounted samurai and those of their retainers on foot that could keep up with the breakneck pace. Other units had to try to follow up as fast as they could.

On more orderly, regular marches the vanguard was of crucial importance as these troops had to screen the main force against attacks as well as scout and to find and prepare suitable places for establishing camp. In addition to regular units a small number of nimble and nifty men acted as *teisatsu* or spies/scouts.

The large illustration provided on the preceding pages shows a complete unit of the Sakai clan army on the march around 1700. The Sakai were daimyo in Maebashi (Kosuke Province, today's Gunma Prefecture), 100 km to the NW from Edo/Tokyo, and old supporters *(fudai)* of the Tokugawa. They enjoyed an annual income of 125.000 koku in 1749, which secured them a comfortable position among the middle group of daimyo. Their military strength was then assessed as 5876 men with 928 horses. However, 1759 men out of this total were not samurai or ashigaru but were recruited from the peasant population to serve as auxiliaries. 573 of the horses also came from the countryside and were used to transport supplies and equipment. This practice of recruiting men and animals for wartime auxiliary service had its roots way back in the past even before the Sengoku Period, when the Takeda, for example, had a clear-cut system in which military support service could replace tax payments.

The Sakai forces were divided into nine units (*sonae*). Seven of these battalion-sized, combined arms units were under the command of *karo*, leading vassals of the House of Sakai who fought under their own personal standards. The eighth unit was called *hatamoto-sonae*, comprising the direct vassals (*hatamoto*) of the daimyo and thus serving as his core, elite unit. The ninth sonae belonged to the next-in-line to the daimyo, usually his eldest son. It was called *wakatono-sama-sonae* ("wakatono" meaning "young lord"). All nine units comprised roughly the same types of troops and numbers, only the lord's own sonae was slightly larger in numbers.

The illustration represents the *sonae* belonging to one of the Sakai *karo*, Honda Minbuzaemon, who also held the purely military rank of samurai daisho. The unit is on the march numbering 365 men with 54 horses. At least 107 of the total are civilian auxiliaries: 86 *ninzoku*, mostly employed to act as personal attendants to mounted samurai, and 21 *kuchitori* who were pack horse drivers. As for its combat elements, Honda's unit has all the classical weapon types concentrated in their own sub-units: mounted samurai, long pikes, bows, and guns. It is in fact a small, but tactically complete and self-sustained mixed-weapon combat group, which was not different from the ones fielded in the preceding Sengoku Period (see the foldout pages for a graphic representation of this unit).

Main Gate of Kochi Castle

The mighty *Ote-mon* (main gate) of Kochi Castle stands in stark contrast to the rough field fortification shown before. Kochi was the main castle town of the Chosokabe daimyo family in Tosa Province (today's Kochi Prefecture in Shikoku). This gate was built between 1601 and 1611 by the new daimyo replacing the Chosokabe after Sekigahara, Yamauchi Kazutoyo, together with other well-preserved structures at Kochi Castle. The location of the early 17th century castle is the Otakasa Hill which used to be very swampy. The Chosokabe had not been able to build a castle on this exact spot.

Pack horses

1 Wooden frame for a pack horse, a: seen from the front; b: from the side; c: from behind.
The horse's back is protected from chafing by a thick cushion stuffed with straw which was placed under a leather cover directly under the wooden frame. Between the frame and the baggage there was often a straw mat. Hamamatsu Castle Museum owns a finely decorated example of a complete packsaddle, with a red leather cover, black lacquered wood and metal fittings. Such luxury indicates that the Hamamatsu saddle was used for a daimyo's ceremonial journey to Edo; in the Sengoku Period such saddles were made of undecorated materials and the wooden parts were simply lashed together.

2–6 Pack horses with various baggage containers.
Containers were made in various shapes from freshly cut greenish *igusa* straw or rattan. There were plenty of mats, cloth curtains, other textiles, tools and camp utensils to be transported. The horse's belly was often protected by a broad apron made of thick cloth or straw. A tightly wrapped apron could replace the abdominal belt, and it was also a place where military badges or *mon* were displayed (**Fig. 4**: Honda, **Fig. 6**: Takeda). Ropes used with pack horses could be made of dried stems of the taro plant and stewed with *miso* (salty, fermented soy bean paste). In case of need, spare ropes could be cut up and boiled in water, resulting in a nourishing soup. Discarded rice bale lids made of straw that were not used any longer could also be cut up and used to make porridge for the horses.

7 Marking flags for pack horses. Horses in baggage trains were often marked by small flags erected on top of the saddle. The flags could either generally indicate the daimyo/commander to whom the horse and its cargo belonged (**Fig. 2, 5–7),** or indicate a sub-unit within an army whose baggage the horse carried (**Fig. 3**). **Fig. 7** is taken from a pictorial scroll in Shinjuku Historical Museum (Tokyo), which shows a baggage train belonging to the Naito, old supporters of the Tokugawa. As their small pack train flags the Naito did not chose their main mon, which was a richly detailed, stylized depiction of the Chinese wisteria but the numeral character *ju, meaning* "ten", in a circle. This would have been much more visible and recognizable in this small size.

8a, b Horse shoes made of straw

Honda Minbuzaemon´s Unit on the March, c. 1700
(see also the foldout pages)

Banner Unit

hata-bugyo	1 commander of banner-bearer unit (staff rank)
nori'uma	1 horse for riding
ninzoku	5 auxiliaries
hatasashi = kachi no ashigaru	9 banner- or flag-bearers (foot soldiers)
ko-gashira	1 NCO („corporal")
shogimochi	3 porters of foldable camp stools
matoi-umajirushi-mochi = kachi no ashigaru	6 bearers of large standards (foot soldiers)
shogimochi	2 porters of foldable camp stools
dogumochi-ninzoku	4 porters of weapons/tools
bu'uma, bumma	1 pack horse
kuchitori	1 horse driver

The first group comprises the banner-bearers under the *hata-bugyo*. Right in front and visible from afar come the *nobori* rectangular long banners which were also used to signal. These banners show the *kamon* (coat of arms) of Lord Sakai as they were military instruments, not personal standards. Next are the two personal standards of Honda Minbuzaemon *(uma-jirushi)*. Large banners and standards required more than one carrier. Since Minbuzaemon hailed from the famous and wide-spread Honda family their crest appears on one of his personal standards. The banner unit would arrive first at any camp or rest site and mark the area using the banners, with Honda´s personal banners placed to indicate where the centre of his camp would be set up. Folded camp stools are included with this group to allow senior officers to sit down without any delay once they have reached the prepared rest area. The rear of the banner group is brought up by its leader, surrounded by his arms carriers and other attendants. The bigger and better equipped the group of personal retainers surrounding their mounted master was, the more respectable he appeared to everybody standing or kneeling at the side of the road.

First and Second Combat Units (Teppo-tai x2)

teppo-gashira	1 officer of teppo handgunners x2
nori'uma	1 horse for riding x2
ninzoku	5 auxiliaries x2
teppo-ashigaru	36 foot soldiers with arquebus x2
tamagusuribako-mochi	2 porters of the chest for gunpowder and balls x2
gusoku-kawago-mochi	6 basket porters for armour x2
kodogu-mochi	3 porters of tool boxes x2
bu'uma, bumma	2 pack horses x2
kuchitori	2 horse drivers x2

Next come the two ashigaru teppo units, each with 36 arquebusiers. Their mounted commanders (*teppo-gashira*) are in the van, the gunners´ own small supply unit in the rear. If war was imminent, transport would most likely be beefed up to carry more powder and shot.

Long-Pike-Ashigaru

nagae-bugyo	1 officer of long pikes holding staff rank
nori'uma	1 horse for riding
ninzoku	2 auxiliaries
nagae-ashigaru	30 foot soldiers with long pikes
dogumochi	3 porters of tool boxes
bu'uma, bumma	2 pack horses
kuchitori	2 horse drivers

Fourth in the marching order is an element comprising 30 ashigaru with long pikes (*nagae-yari*) led by their mounted bugyo. Some supplies are transported at the rear. A bugyo always out-ranked a kashira which is an indication of the elite status of ashigaru with long yari.

Mounted Samurai

kishi	22 mounted samurai
noriuma	22 horses for riding
ninzoku	58 auxiliaries on foot

The most stretched-out element is the *kishi-tai* (literally "unit of knights", i.e. mounted samurai and their retainers) on position No.5. The leader has a retinue of nine; the other samurai are served by two or three auxiliaries each.

Headquarters Unit

gungen	2 staff officers
nori'uma	2 horses for riding
ninzoku	5 auxiliaries
kachi-metsuke	1 provost
odaiko	1 large drum
kaiyaku	1 conch trumpet blower
taikomochi	2 drum porters
kaimochi	1 carrier of conch trumpet
bu'uma, bumma	1 pack horse
kuchitori	1 horse driver

After the mounted unit a small headquarters troop follows, led by two mounted *gungen* (staff officers), including the provost (*kachi-metsuke*) and four men to carry and operate the big drum and conch trumpet. "Kachi" in *metsuke* indicates that the provost was only supervising those equipped with armour from the arsenal, i.e. ashigaru; samurai were supervised by a higher-ranking *o-metsuke* working directly under the daimyo.

Commander and Retinue

samurai-daisho	1 samurai unit commander
nori'uma	1 horse for riding
ashigaru	38 foot soldiers
bu'uma, bumma	6 pack horses
kuchitori	6 horse drivers

On position No.7 follows the *sonae* commander Honda Minbuzaemon himself, ranked as *samurai-daisho*. It would have been easy to recognize him, not only because of his splendid armour and the large number of accompanying retainers on foot, but also because he wears his own arms on his sashimono, not the Sakai mon like his other samurai. He has 38 ashigaru following him, marked in small groups by identical sashimono. These foot soldiers were well-armoured and most likely had a high degree of uniformity in their outfit. It is not clear whether they had only swords or also carried a lance.

Archers (Rear Combat Unit)

shingari-yumi-gashira	1 officer of archers; *shingari* meaning "last combat unit"
nori'uma	1 horse for officer
ninzoku	4 auxiliaries
yumi-ashigaru	19 footsoldiers with long bows
yabakomochi	2 quiver carriers
dogumochi	3 equipment carriers
bu'uma, bumma	1 pack horse
kuchitori	1 horse driver

The last combat element before the supply train is the archers unit, with 19 archers led by a mounted kashira, in addition to their own 6-men supply team at the rear. Looking at Honda's sonae in total, there are almost 4 handgunners to each archer (72:19), which practically reverses the earlier proportions at the middle of the 16th century.

Supply Train (*konida*)

konida-bugyo	1 supply and baggage train commander (staff rank)
kashi'uma	1 horse for commander
ninzoku	2 auxiliaries
ashigaru	4 footsoldiers
bu'uma, bumma	8 pack horses
kuchitori	8 horse drivers

The supply train is the last and ninth element of the marching order. It is small, but nevertheless led by a staff-ranked officer, the *konida-bugyo*. The limited amount of supplies carried by his small number of men and horses indicates that Edo Period daimyo were certain to find prepared food, drink and fodder at inns along the way; in the Sengoku Period, it would often have been necessary to carry more supplies.

The sources for the Honda sonae in the Sakai clan army date from c. 1700. However, a unit of similar size in the Sengoku Period would not have looked that much different. In case the march was taking place in enemy territory, units or parts of units might have been detached to lead the way, or to secure the flanks or the supply train; also, the order of marching would have been adapted to circumstances. There would have been fewer handgunners, but more archers and ashigaru with lances; perhaps also a few more mounted samurai.

Command baton (*gunbai*)

Most likely a former possession of the Takeda family. Batons such as this had to be seen by many men when raised on the battlefield, so they were well crafted and decorated with auspicious motives such as *matsu* pines, the moon, the sun, various constellations, meaningful *kanji* or Sanskrit characters.

In Camp

The most important materials used to construct a camp were, apart from locally sourced wood, *tatami* mats and *maku* lengths of cloth. Tatami were made of *igusa* (rush straw) and came in various sizes besides the standard c. 1 x 1.8 metres. Tatami mats were used to provide dry ground to sleep on and they could be folded for use as blankets, cushions, seating mats etc. Maku usually measured c. 2 x 6 metres. They were not always in a natural whitish hue but could by dyed or decorated with bands, stripes and the arms of the lord whose camp they marked. Maku could be tied to iron poles, also transported by the baggage train. The poles were rammed into the ground to form an enclosed rectangular area. A proper *honjin* (headquarters) was thus protected from gusts of wind and also from trespassers and prying eyes. Sometimes the entry area into the maku enclosure was made more prominent by adding a simple construction made of wooden beams or cut trees.

Inside the honjin area observing protocol was vital, and even dirty and tired samurai tried to behave adequately in the presence of their commander. Etiquette followed protocol rules that could be seen on full display at occasions such as the ceremonial banquets before or after battles, or the ritual viewing of heads taken from or rather off the enemy. The area enclosed by maku became so much synonymous with samurai leadership that the samurai-led shogunal government of the Edo Period was usually called *bakufu*, including the word maku in an alternative reading.

The maku area in the field only served as sleeping quarters for the commander and his senior officers when no solid building was available. Even in the 16th century much of Japan was densely populated, included many temples whose buildings could be confiscated for use by the top brass, who had them cordoned off by maku. Lesser members of the army slept less well. Regular tents were unknown at the time, but a samurai who had a length of maku cloth could have a small area cordoned off and have his rest inside with some privacy. In inclement weather his attendants could construct a simple gabled roof from maku or beams or both, which overhung the "walls" keeping out rain water. The floor was to be covered with mats. Low-ranking samurai and ashigaru had to resort to simpler means to reduce the undesirable effects of bad weather. Typically, some earth was dug out to form a pit in which one or a handful of men could sit and sleep under a simple roof made of wood, wicker, and everything else that was available.

Armies also carried large wooden pavises called tate. These could be used for almost anything, from protecting the honjin as a mobile wall, as conference or dinner tables, to provide watertight floorboards or to make the roofs of samurai field quarters more solid. Folding stools and transport boxes provided seating. Banners marked the quarters of commanders and sub-commanders. The baggage train also provided wooden and iron tools for building camp fires and cooking rice. If the army stayed longer, wooden fences would be built, moats dug out and earthen ramparts erected. Key points like rough gates or watch towers were built from locally available wood. When an army prepared to conduct a long siege, huge fortified lines and entire wooden towns shot up in short time, as witnessed outside of Osaka in 1614/15 and at Shimabara in 1637/38.

Right side: Signaling Equipment
At Ishida Mitsunari´s Headquarters, Sekigahara Reenactment, 2000

Ashigaru serving as signallers have readied their equipment inside the HQ, which is cordoned off by *maku* cloth curtains. One method used to give signals that could be seen from far away was generating smoke by burning various types of wood, twigs, grass, pine branches, straw and charcoal in a kettle. Shape and colour of the smoke emitted would tell those familiar with the code its message. The lower picture shows a battery of bamboo tubes set up to launch signal rockets, which could be used to transmit faster signals. The rack in front is built to hold yari lances.

83

Painted screen (byobu) showing the army besieging Osaka Castle in 1614/15

Individual units all have their own protected camps. Inside the enclosures there are small thatched sheds built of wood and mud as living quarters. Walls, towers and gates are made of wooden planks, unhewn wood, wicker, and wooden shingles. (Osaka Castle Museum)

There are no handbooks for accommodation in the field from the Sengoku Period, but the source *Gunyo Senkou Zukai* from 1708 provides detailed information (published and translated by www.samuraibookshop.com).
The most basic form of protection for resting troops consists of three trees bent back to form arches. These are reenforced with horizontal pieces of wood or bamboo. The area under the arches is then covered with rough mats, branches, twigs, or whatever is available.

Basic protection for troops in the field
(Gunyo Senkou Zukai, 1708)

Camp layout according to *Gunyo Senkou Zukai*

The small dots represent men housed in the sheds before which they gather ready to march off. The large numbers of men before the samurai sheds are not all samurai but include their attendants and often horses, too.

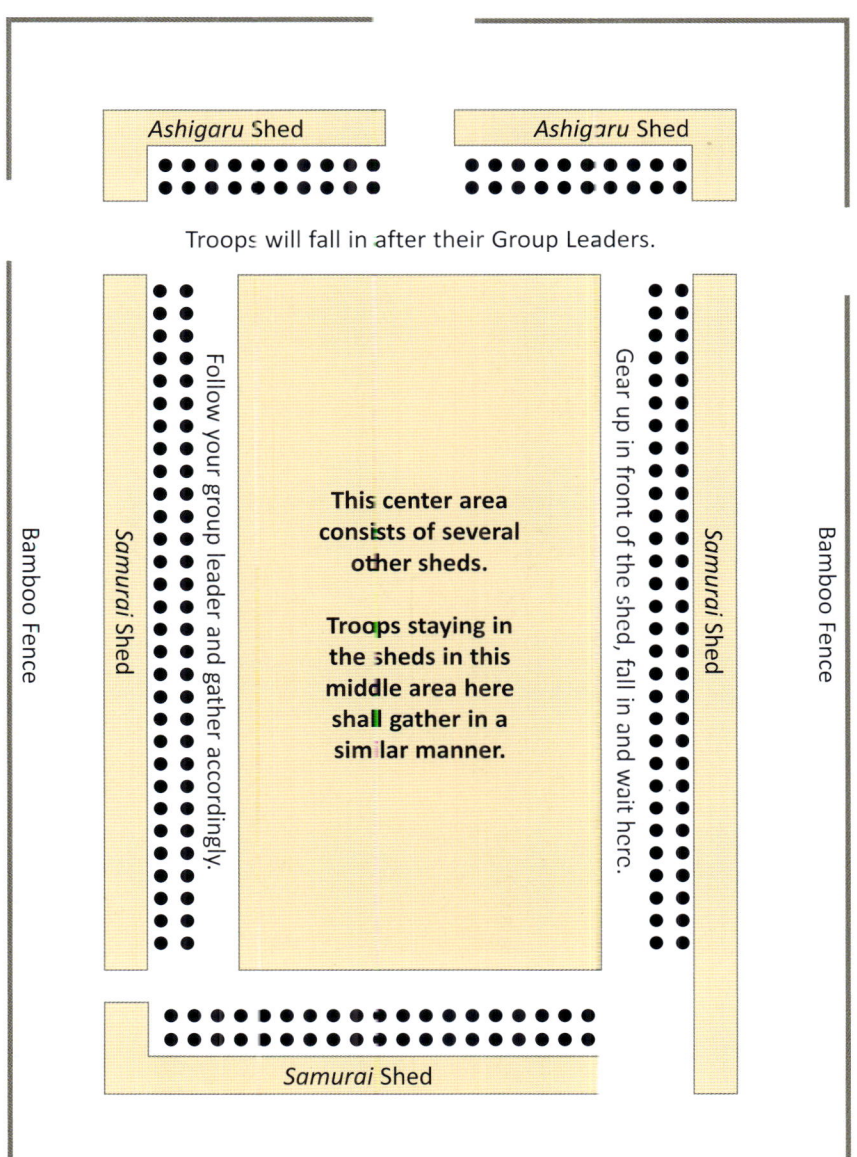

According to *Gunyo Senkou Zukai* a more substantial camp should be surrounded by a fence made of crossed bamboo poles, leaving six openings. Inside there are numerous *koya* (huts or sheds) for units of samurai and ashigaru and their horses. These quarters surround one central area which has even more sheds. To enlarge the camp, more rows of sheds could be added in a rectangular pattern. Rows of sheds should have at least 3 ken (5.45 m) between them unless they stood back to back, in which case 1 ken was deemed sufficient. Between the fence and the first row of sheds inside the camp there should be 5 or 6 ken (c. 10 m).

Even as samurai, their retainers and groups of ashigaru lived close to each other, social distinctions remained. Ashigaru sheds were occupied assuming that 2 tsubo (6.6 square meters) were sufficient space for three men.

However, mounted samurai had as much space to themselves as six of their retainers or their horse.

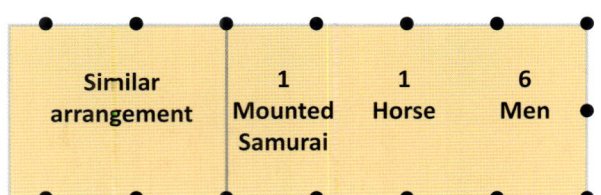

Shed arranged for a mounted samurai and his retainers. Their quarters are marked by eleven posts rammed into the ground, similar quarters are on one side. The covered area is 10.8 x 5.4 m and should also hold baggage and anything else that should not be exposed to the elements. One area in which Japan bested contemporary European

Based on similar principles but much more comfortable were permanent barracks quarters which could be found inside newer castles of the Sengoku Period. The quarters shown here are *nagaya* (combining the characters for "long" and "place" or "house"): a row of small rooms for men, interspersed with rooms for horses and equipment. In this *de luxe* version in Aizu Wakamatsu the roof is tiled, and there is a paved and covered walkway. The small room on the next page has a neat tatami floor and should have housed about three unmarried men. This example is from the late Edo Period where living quarters even at humble dwellings were generally built raised from the ground, leaving a small, lower space at the entrance for getting in or out of one´s footwear *(genkan)*. This architectural trend which protected the population (and soldiers) from the damp and dirty ground contributed much to a better lifestyle; in the Sengoku Period it was not yet universal. (Saigo Tanomo Residence in Aizu Wakamatsu)

armies was hygiene. To allow the men to relieve themselves in the safety of the camp but with minimum molestation for everybody, a copious number of pits covered with planks were dug along the back sides of sheds. The back sides were to have no windows or doors, so the camps were much healthier than in Europe.

Gunyo Senkou Zukai does not provide much information on how the sheds were built. Sometimes they only consisted of posts (either brought by the baggage train or locally cut down) and a thatched roof, mats, tree branches with leaves, or in case of a longer period of stay, wooden shingles. If possible, the back sides were closed off using wood. The ground consisted of rammed earth and was covered with mats or straw. The front side typically remained open as the men lived as much in front of their sheds as inside. Of course, some samurai had their own maku cloth curtains and used them to gain protection, privacy, and prestige.

Shed occupied by samurai displaying a mon (coat of arms) on the maku curtains.

Samurai who did not have a banner of their own had retainers carry their helmets or sheathed yari lances to indicate their masters' presence. Lance points here are covered by decorated covers (*yari saya* – more about standards and heraldic displays in volume 2). The rectangular flag and the object including two furry red balls are sashimono back flags belonging to individual samurai. (*Gunyo Senkou Zukai*)

In Battle – Sengoku Period Tactics

When designing their battle plans, samurai army commanders made sure that their troops remained as mobile and flexible as possible, even when formed up. Often there were no precise battle plans for pre-determined tactical movements. Instead there was a number of known and less-well known or even secret basic formations which were adapted according to circumstances. These were employed taking into consideration the terrain, weather, one's own and enemy strength and the overall goal of the battle, which did not simply have to be to decimate the enemy as much as possible. Troops were trained and organized in different units determined by weapon types, but now they had to fight together to maximize the capabilities of each branch of the army.

Some authors claim that formulating battle tactics only became important in the Edo Period, mostly as a theoretical exercise, and that most Sengoku battle plans were simply determined by everybody's desire to close with the enemy as quickly as possible and start a wild melee en masse. Apparent visual arguments supporting this view are preserved painted wooden screens called *byobu* which mostly show messy groups of charging troops and heroic fights involving individual samurai. Most of these battle scenes show very little tactical coordination. Mostly painted in the 17th century, the byobu simply follow time-honoured narrative conventions handed down in samurai-related arts including literature and illustration. The heroic and individualistic element in samurai warfare had already become an anachronism in the mass battles of the Sengoku Period which had, by the 16th century, produced a highly sophisticated and effective war machine. Of course, there were books on tactics such as the "Eight Formations" (*hachijin*) coming from Tang Period China. These classics were well-known in Japan, and some Sengoku Period samurai studied them. Some clans employed respected military strategists who developed methods to use their masters' armies to their full potential. There are other facts to take into account when doubting the reality of samurai warfare as shown by most *byobu*: Why should a daimyo detach up to 10% of his fighting men as communications specialists (messengers, signallers, banner units, scouts) if all he wanted was to hack away at a mass of enemies? The Uesugi for instance had 402 men alone carrying banners in their army of 6871. Naturally the general's intentions were to remain in full control of everything happening before, during and after battle, and he needed these specialists to influence events on the battlefield by relaying his orders as efficiently as possible.

Another reason why tactical information written in the Sengoku Period is so rare is that the most advanced ideas and practices were of course military secrets which were collected and occasionally recorded only in the more peaceful Edo Period when the fighting was actually over. This information served to support the tendency to preserve for future generations the military skills that had been proven

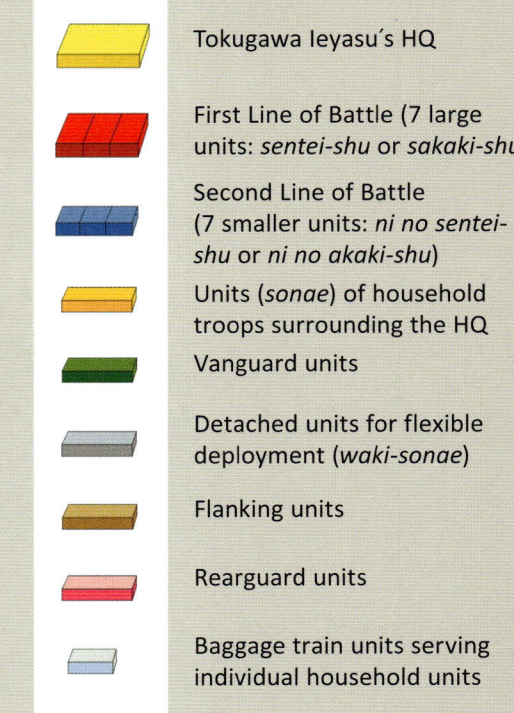

Tokugawa Ieyasu's HQ

First Line of Battle (7 large units: *sentei-shu* or *sakaki-shu*)

Second Line of Battle (7 smaller units: *ni no sentei-shu* or *ni no akaki-shu*)

Units (*sonae*) of household troops surrounding the HQ

Vanguard units

Detached units for flexible deployment (*waki-sonae*)

Flanking units

Rearguard units

Baggage train units serving individual household units

Ideal Deployment of Tokugawa Ieyasu's Grand Army

Ieyasu (1542–1616) combined his own Tokugawa household troops with those of allied and subordinate commanders. The latter had their contingents placed in the first and second lines of battle (at Tennoji in 1615 there were even three such battle lines) and would bear the brunt of the fighting suffering the highest number of casualties, while Ieyasu retained overall command and observed their performance. Still, positions in the front lines were much sought-after because they offered opportunities to prove loyalty and gain glory and rewards under the eyes of the supreme commander. In addition, Tokugawa Ieyasu fielded 20 units of his own troops. These occupied altogether safer positions, guarding his HQ on all sides and providing flexible, fast response capabilities. Household troops were in fact deployed like a separate army within a larger army, with their own vanguard, rearguard and flanking units.

Ieyasu was able to use natural rivalries between his allies and subordinates to maximize fighting spirit and morale, but also to maintain personal security, stability and control with troops ready to be used wherever and whenever he deemed their intervention useful. An elaborate intelligence-gathering and communication system was in place to maintain his ability to control and com- mand even when six-digit numbers of warriors clashed or weather conditions were inclement.

Our ideal deployment features 20 Tokugawa household units (*sonae*) and 14 contingents led by others. Just to give an idea of numerical dimensions – the first battle lines at Sekigahara in 1600 contained 15 contingents led by subordinate generals, varying in strength from 500 to 6000 men, making the army a total of 44,280 men. Contingents from the back lines did not hesitate to resort to trickery to move up and join the fight as early as possible. Tokugawa household troops at Sekiga- hara numbered 30,000 in 20 units. Some of these men did not fight at all, but their presence was as essential to the final victory as the fighting spirit of the front-line contingents and the Kobayakawa treason.

The system shown is only basic and would have been adapted to varying situations. At Sekigahara there were another five units with a total of 14,528 men, led by other subordinate generals. These were deployed to safeguard the vulnerable left flank of the Tokugawa, covering it from the rear up, as there were enemy units in the area whose behaviour was hard to predict. This brought the total strength of Ieyasu's army at Sekigahara to slightly under 89,000.

(Sekigahara troop figures from: *Zusetsu. Sengoku Kassen Chizu-shu*, p. 140-1)

winners and instrumental in shaping the outcome of the turbulent Sengoku Period – blueprints for success. This means that again many documents including chronicles, handbooks and some pictorial materials from the 17th and even 18th centuries are important sources also for studying Sengoku military history.

Among known tactical base formations there are some that appear hard to grasp at first sight. The formations look much lighter and with much bigger spaces between units than it would have been the case in 16th/17th century Europe. There was a large amount of flexibility in Japan when it came to dividing and subdividing units, and the number of lines, blocks, circles and other shapes in the plans seems potentially infinite. The most basic subdivision usually included a vanguard (*zengun*), a middle guard or main force (*chugun*), and a rearguard (*sente, chosei, atozume*), right and left wing flanking units, as well as flexible response units (*yusei* or *yugun*). Among basic principles that emerge from studying the old battle plans is the standard positioning of specialized ashigaru units with bows, guns, and long pikes in the front and flank lines. This seems to be decidedly unheroic, but it was the humble foot soldiers who had the power to stop or slow down enemy attacks, and pragmatism in this case won over the romanticized world of the *byobu*. The job of the samurai units was to finish off the attackers once they had been slowed down, or to go on the offensive themselves. The most mobile units were mounted samurai who were kept in positions that allowed for fast attacks in various directions. The most prestigious units formed by the *hatamoto* were close to the commander's headquarters, usually in the centre of the formation, often slightly oriented towards the rear.

Headquarters: *Maku* Cloth Curtains

The site selected for an HQ was marked by ramming iron poles into the ground, between which lengths of cloth (*maku*) were strung up to create an enclosure. To keep *maku* in their wall-like shape they had straps sewn on their upside through which a tight rope was led.

1. An open maku front, sporting the Tokugawas' *aoi no mon* (triple hollyhock) which was usually given in blue or black on white ground.
2. Maku could be monochrome, sport stripes of various colours or be adorned by mon. These are the maku around Uesugi Kenshin's HQ at Kawanakajima in 1561 (see original pictorial source on p. 94). However, the artist presented both mon more elaborately than they actually were by increasing the number of parts of the chrysanthemum and the number of umbels of the paulownia mon. This reconstruction gives correct heraldic detail.
3. A large army such as that fielded by Tokugawa Ieyasu did not have just one HQ area cordoned off by maku. The Tokugawa used maku with white and blue stripes at least at the battles of the Anegawa (1570) and Sekigahara (1600).
4. Single piece of a maku "wall" with a samurai figure for scale. There were many small slits in the cloth, not only to permit vision but also to weaken the impact of wind on the fabric.
5. Rectangular, basic maku HQ. The ground inside was often covered with straw, mats or wooden *tate* pavises. The basic shape could be easily adapted to various terrains and incorporate existing small buildings and trees. More elaborate wooden gateways could be built, *tate*, rows of spikes and moats could be added to enhance security. Furthermore, more maku cloth and beams could be used to construct a gabled roof over parts of the HQ.

Examples for *horo* Variants

1. Horo with three black *fuku-nuki* banners (streamers), worn by Ohara Kyuzo, vassal to the Hosokawa. This would have looked spectacular when worn by a fast-moving mounted warrior.
2. Toyotomi Hideyoshi's tsukaiban (mounted messenger corps). The horo is gold, while the flag sports a large Toyotomi *kamon* over a smaller *mon* which is the personal crest of the samurai.
3. Tsukai-ban belonging to Sakakibara Yasukatsu's (1590–1615) troops.
4. Tsukai-ban belonging to Todo Takatora's (1556–1630) troops. There is also another variant of a red and black cloth horo. The small golden fan mounted on the staff is the personal mark of an individual samurai.
5. Matsudaira Tadaaki's (1583–1644) tsukai-ban. He used the golden diamond motive for all his banners and flags.

For further information on horo, see pp. 44 & 103.

Headquarters: *Honjin* Personnel

1. Supreme commander's personal standards
2. Nobori banners used for signalling
3. The supreme commander
4. Personal Retainers
5. Valet holding the supreme commander's sword, and weapon carriers to the lord
6. *Gunshi* or *gun-bugyo* (chief of staff or chief adviser)
7. Clerk with low table
8. Sub-commanders or staff officers
9. Conch trumpet and signal drums with crew
10. Doctors, priests, assistants
11. Mounted messengers (tsukai-ban)
12. Horses to the tsukai-ban
13. Lifeguards samurai
14. Other HQ troops
15. Various support troops
16. Maku enclosure

Uesugi Kenshin´s headquarters before the Fourth Battle of Kawanakajima in 1561
Scene from a painted screen named "Kawanakajima kassen-zu byobu" at the Uesugi Museum in Yonezawa, Yamagata Prefecture

This *honjin* has been erected in a depression in the terrain surrounded by hills. It is protected both by maku and wooden fences. Lord Uesugi is sitting on a camp stool placed on straw mats, with a roof made of wood and straw protecting him from the elements. A group of staff officers led by the strategist Usami Sadayuki (1539–1599) is kneeling in attendance. Other HQ staff including several banner bearers are outside of the maku enclosure (see p. 90 for a discussion of maku crests)..

A Standard Basic Unit Reconstructed (pp. 98–99)

To sum up the facts provided regarding structure of command, troop types, numerical strength, and tactical deployment introduced above we now attempt to reconstruct an archetypical formation of a generic small clan army or sub unit *(sonae)* of a larger army. The time is the last decades of the 16th century until early in the 17th c., assumed strength is 1100 men. The formation chosen is relatively simple and shows the army in basic layout, with strongly protected headquarters. It could be expected to speedily adopt another formation for more specific purposes such as those presented on the following pages 95–97.

In our reconstruction, staff officers and the cavalry element (lifeguards and mounted samurai) are dismounted, surrounding the commander with their horses held close-by. The sources are various clan´s army lists as well as pictorial records of Takeda, Yamagata, Date, Honda, and Matsuura troops.

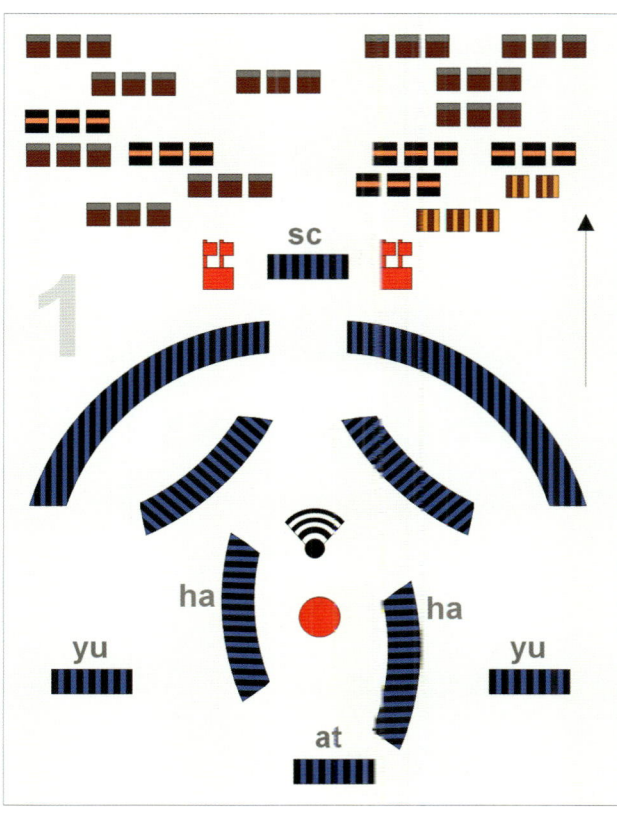
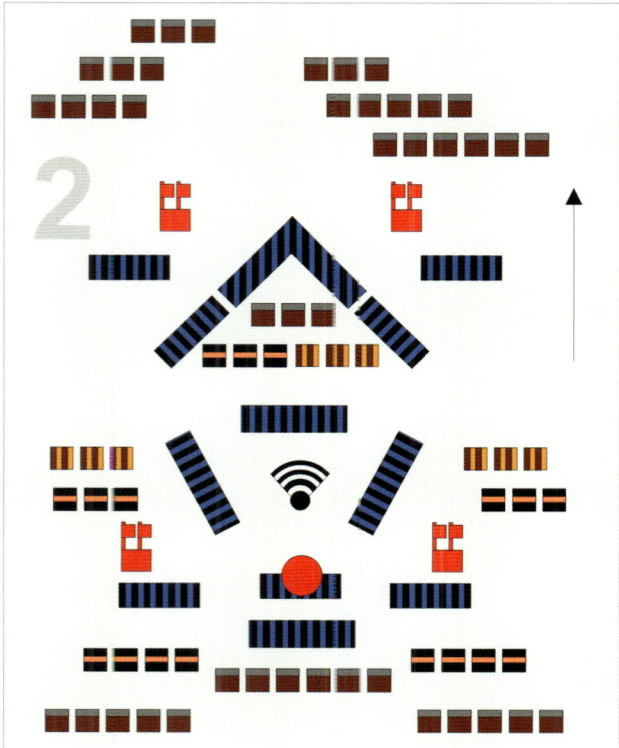
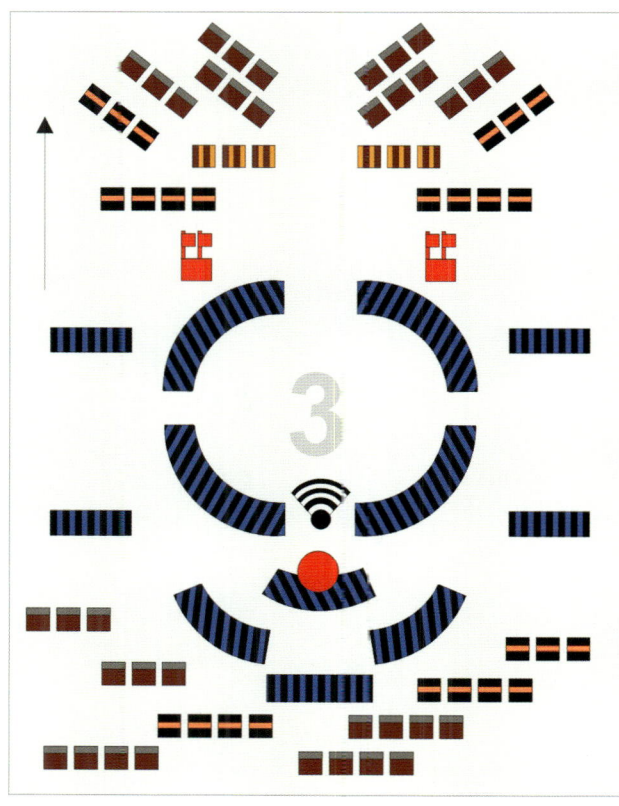

sc Vanguard (*sente chosei*)
ha Household Troops (*hatamoto*)
yu Flexible Reaction Units (*yusei*)
at Rearguard (*atozume*)

**Tactical Formations during the Sengoku Period
A Selection of Nine Basic Variations**

1 ***kakuyoku* (Crane's wings)**
  Purpose: Keeping the balance. Can be easily transformed into an attacking formation.

2 ***hoshi* (Arrowhead)**
  Offensive formation. Provides a strong central punch, useful combating an enemy in fig. 1 formation, the crane's wings.

3 ***hoen* (Circle)**
  All-round defensive formation. Described in the Takeda handbook, the *Koyo Gunkan*.

(Source: *Senryaku Senjutsu Heiki*
(Weapons, Strategy, Tactics 2), pp. 34–37)

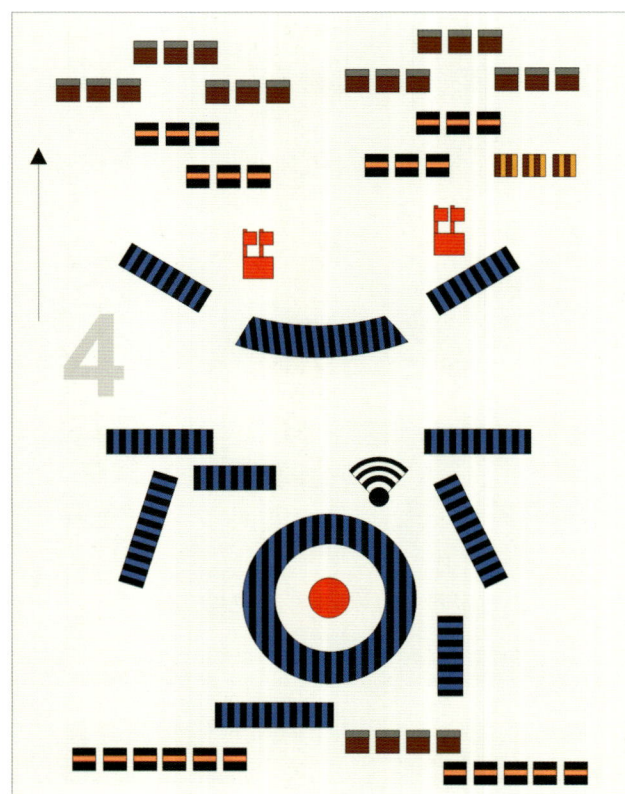
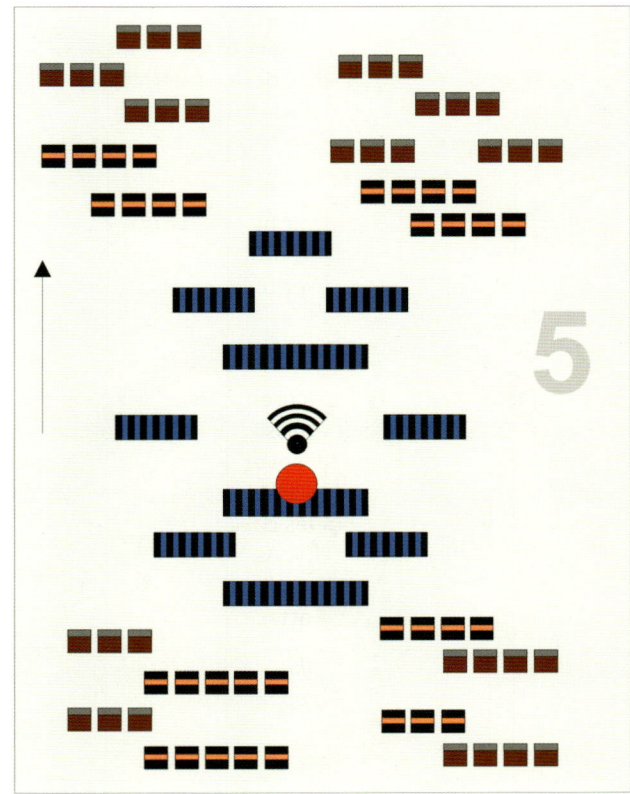
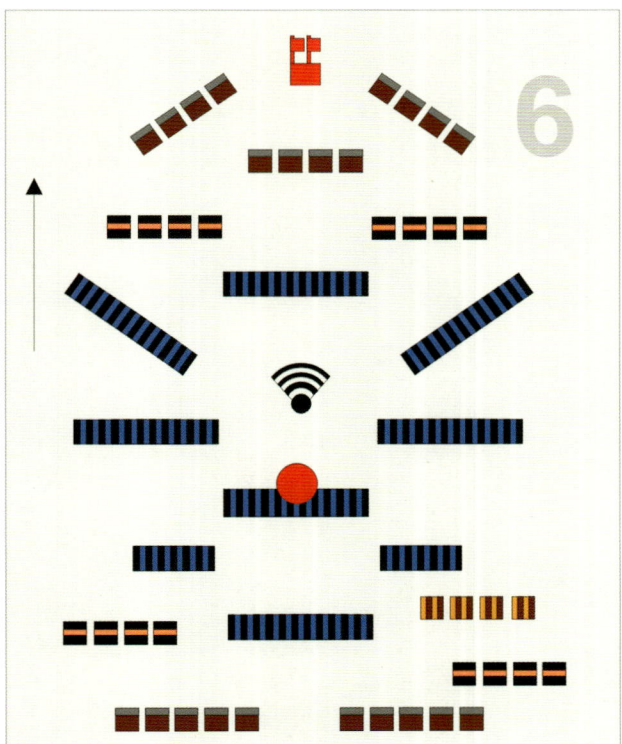

Tactical Formations during the Sengoku Period

A Selection of Nine Basic Variations

4 koyaku (Oxen yoke)
Purpose: Defending against formation No. 2, the Arrowhead. The attacker will be encircled by a "yoke" and then attacked in the flanks by troops stationed close to the HQ.

5 ganko (Swarm of wild geese)
Purpose: Offensive while maintaining strong security on all flanks. Units able to "swarm" the enemy guarantee for a high degree of flexibility.

6 koto (Tiger head)
Purpose: strong offensive potential spearheaded by wedge formation. Uesugi Kenshin countered the Tiger head by deploy- ing in formation No. 5.

7 kurumagakari (cart´s wheel)
Purpose: Constant attacks against one point in the enemy line until it breaks. Units or pairs of units move up the spiral, attack and withdraw fast, to be replaced by following units. Enemy will be worn down while constantly rotating attackers are only

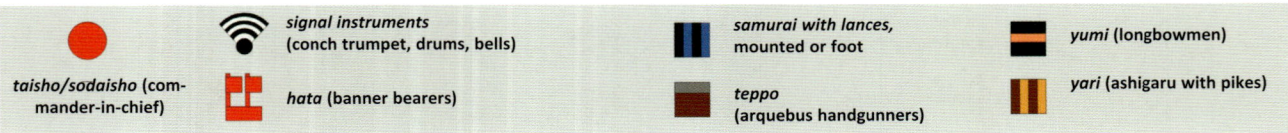

briefly engaged. The army is an ever-moving spiral of units with the commander in its centre. This formation was famously deployed by Uesugi Kenshin in 1561 against Takeda Shingen's crane's wings (fig. 1).

8   *ryukei* (Flowing form)
Purpose: Orderly retreat unit by unit. One by one, units attack enemy who has broken through. At the same time, HQ and other units can "flow" away towards the rear.

9   *matsukawa* (Pine bark)
Purpose: Defense. HQ is secured by an inner ring of lifeguard samurai, with missile and yari troops deployed outside. Samurai cover all sides, with foot samurai on the inside, and mounted troops on the outside. This provides cover for the core but also gives great mobility. As the formation is extremely hard to pin down, the enemy will think twice before mounting an attack.

(Source: Senryaku Senjutsu Heiki Weapons, Strategy, Tactics 2), pp. 84–87)

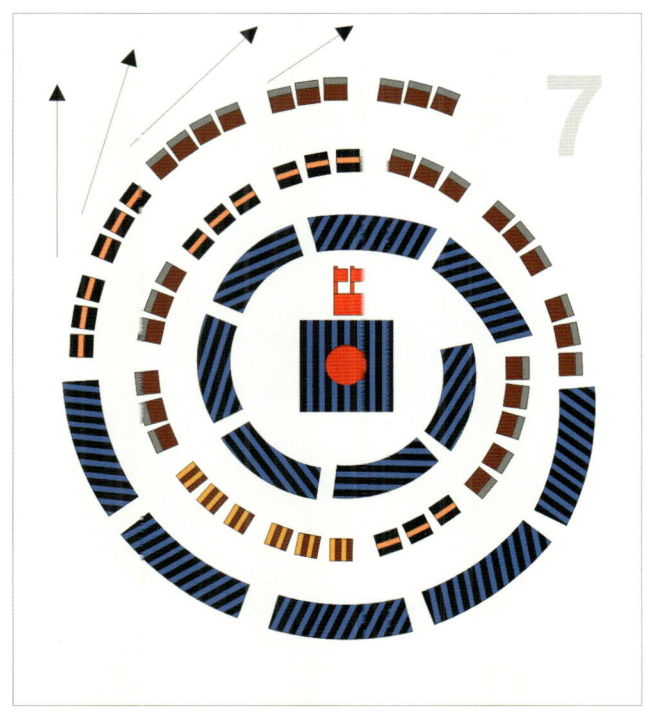

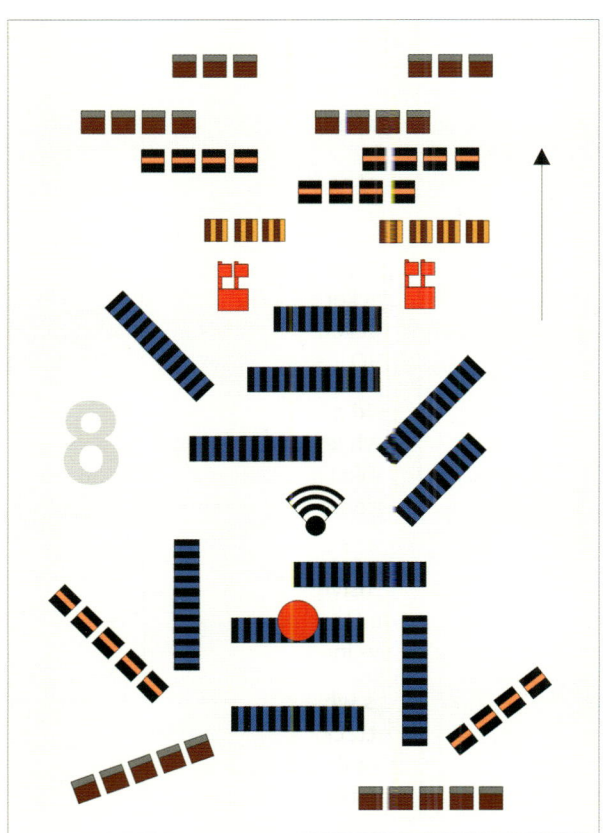

Key to troop types:
Commander-in-chief (mounted): 1
Mounted samurai officers
(bugyo, ashigaru-daisho, metsuke, kumi-gashira): 23
Tsukai-ban (mounted messengers): 4
Umawari-shu (mounted lifeguards): 40
Other mounted samurai: 40
Foot samurai with lance: 150
Ashigaru with lance: 120
Ashigaru with long pike: 90
Missile ashigaru (mixed gun/bow): 125
Samurai or ashigaru in charge of small missile units
(ko-gashira, keigo-yoriki if mounted samurai): 30
Signalers (bannermen, musicians): 41
Foot retainers to mounted samurai officers: 131
(low-ranking samurai, ashigaru, support troops)
Foot retainers to tsukai-ban: 12
Foot retainers (kinju) to other mounted samurai: 162
Porters and horse-drivers: 100
Doctor with assistants, clerks: 5
Total 1094, including approx. 120 mounted

Army composition:
1 Units of 5 missile ashigaru with ko-gashira on foot
2 Ashigaru with long pikes in single rows: 50 facing the enemy, and 20 each on the flanks
3 Units consisting of 30 samurai with lances, backed up by 30 lance ashigaru
4 Banner units of 15 ashigaru each with identical nobori flags
5 15 foot samurai with lances
6 40 dismounted samurai with short lances
7 Umawari-shu: 40 mounted samurai, with 1 personal retainer each
8 10 staff officers and valets to the commander, clerk (camp stools for highest-ranking officers)
9 Commander-in-chief, dismounted on camp stool
10 Commander's horses with retainers
11 Horses to Fig. 6 & 8 with one retainer each
12 Baggage train (various porters, pack horses not illustrated)
13 2 x 2 mounted tsukai-ban with 3 retainers each
14 Conch trumpet (2 signalers)
15 Large drum (3 signalers)
16 O-umajirushi (commander's great personal standard), with 3 carriers
17 Rear standard with 3 carriers
18 Mounted metsuke or kenshi (supervisor, provost) with 2 retainers each
19 Hata-bugyo (staff officer in charge of banners, mounted, 7 retainers)
20 Yari-bugyo (staff officer in command of lance-armed troops, mounted, 7 retainers)
21 Omochi-yari-bugyo (staff officers commanding second contingent of lance-armed troops, mounted, 7 retainers)
22 Nobori-bugyo (staff officer in charge of nobori banners, mounted, 7 retainers)
23 Kumi-gashira (officers commanding ashigaru units, mounted, 5 retainers)
24 Musha-bugyo (staff officer in charge of mounted samurai, mounted, 7 retainers)
25 Another bugyo (staff officer in charge of unit No. 3, mounted, 7 retainers)
26 Ashigaru-daisho (commanders of missile units, mounted, 5 retainers)
27 Medical staff

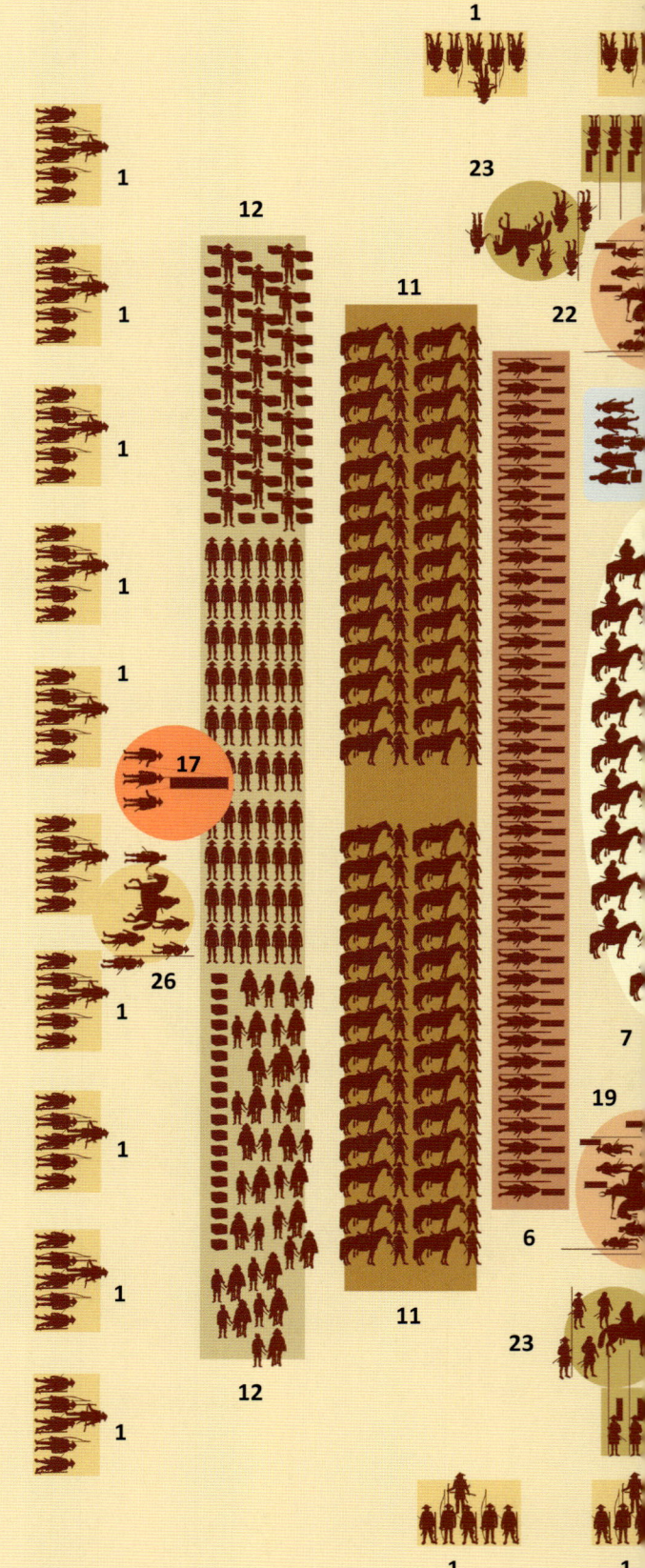

Ideal Basic Formation of a 1100-strong Unit (mid-16th c. through Edo Period)

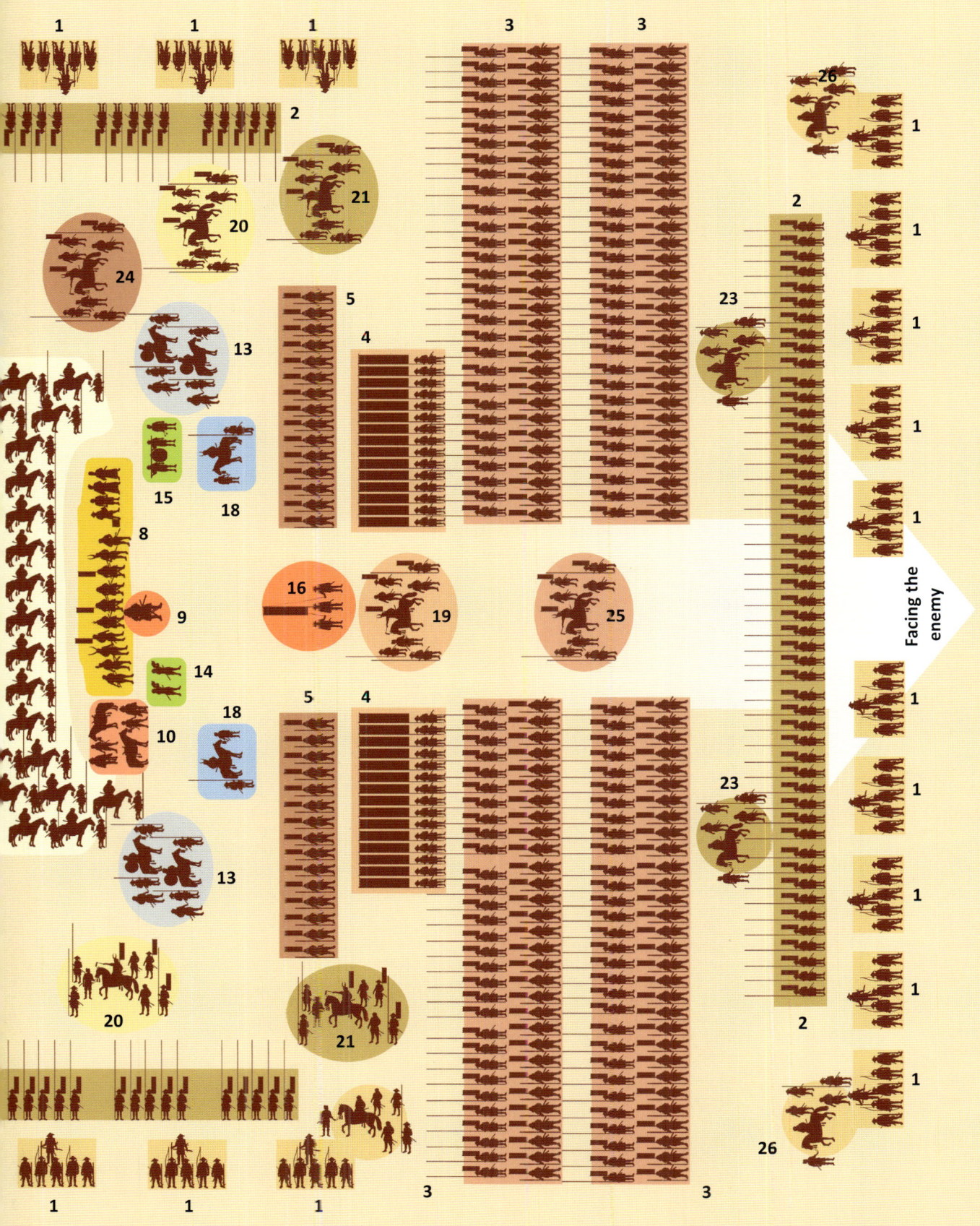

KEY TERMS IN JAPANESE AND ENGLISH

abumi	stirrups made of wood or iron
ai-jirushi	"badge" design displayed on banners or equipment to indicate clan affiliation
ashigaru	"swift feet" (foot soldier class appearing in the 15th century)
ashigaru-daisho	a samurai commanding an ashigaru unit
Azuchi Momoyama Period	a period of great cultural achievements, c. 1568–1603
bamen	wooden or armoured horse's chamfrom
ban	group, unit; in military terms roughly equivalent to a company
bugyo	samurai holding mid- or staff officer rank
chigyochi	rural fief owned by samurai
chugun	main force of an army
daimyo	samurai lord holding his own territory
do	armour, specifically protecting front and back of torso
do-maru	an older type of armour made of many small pieces tied together by cords
dora	a gong
eboshi	soft cap in various shapes
Edo Period	1603–1867
fudai	samurai vassal families who enjoyed the special trust of their lord
gunbai	fan used to command troops
gun-bugyo, gunshi	a senior staff officer giving strategical and tactical advice to the commander (also called sobu-gyo, ikusa-bugyo)
gunkan, gunsha, gunshi	generic terms for samurai staff officers
gusoku	a suit of armour
gusoku-bugyo	a samurai officer in charge of the armour at his lord´s arsenal
haidate	thigh-protecting armour for mounted samurai
hambo, hanbo	armoured mask for the lower half of the face
hara-ate	a simple suit of armour protecting only breast and hips facing the enemy
haramaki-do	"belly wrapper", a type of armour mostly obsolete by the 16th c.
hatamoto	samurai „under the standard" (= a lord´s direct vassals with medium incomes)
Heian Period	794–1185
honjin, jinmaku	military headquarters
horo	a balloon-like cape at the back of an armour, marking elite status or mounted messengers
horoku	military pay or a fief whose value is paid out in cash
hyoshigi	wooden clappers
ichimon	the top group of vassals including the lord´s relatives
iyozane	small metal plates to be joined together to form armour
jingasa	cone-shaped helmet made of metal, wood or leather
jizamurai	rural samurai
jochu, jodai	commander of a castle or fortress
kabukimono	an unruly, individualistic samurai
kabuto	helmet
kachi, okachi	foot samurai
kai, horagai	a conch trumpet
Kamakura Period	1185–1333
kane	bell
karo	a top vassal or house elder serving a daimyo
kasagake	mounted horse archery on rough grounds
kashin	a samurai vassal holding a fief from a lord (kashindan = a lord´s group of vassals)
kashira, -gashira	leader of a small unit
katana, ken	samurai sword
kerai	vassal, feudal retainer to a lord
kiba-gundan	mounted troops
kinju	low-ranking personal retainer
kishi-tai	a unit of mounted samurai
Kofun Period	3rd to 6th c. AD
ko-gashira	the equivalent of a non-commissioned officer of foot soldiers
kogun, atozume	rearguard
koku	about 180 litres of rice, considered sufficient to feed a man for one year. A basic currency in feudal Japan.
konida	supply and baggage train, "small baggage"
kosho	young attendant to a samurai lord ("squire")
kuchitori	horse driver
kumi, -gumi	group; in military terms, roughly a platoon
kuni-shu	a group of rural samurai originating from the same province
kusazuri	armour plates suspended from the hips
kyuba	mounted horse archery
maedate	decoration for the front of a helmet
maku	large lengths of cloth used to curtain off HQ areas
mempo, menpo	armoured face mask
metsuke, ikusa-metsuke, kenshi	scout, provost, samurai „military police inspector"
mon, kamon	coat of arms or crest of a samurai family
monme	1 monme = 3.75 grams. For arquebus, this is roughly calibre 85 mm
Muromachi Period	1336–1573
nagae-yari, nagae	long pike
naginata	sword lance for fighting on foot
nambanjin	"Southern Barbarians" (= Europeans in 16th/17th c. Japan)

namban-kabuto	helmets inspired by European designs or imported, often variants of the morion	sonae, -zonae	a major military unit, approximately a battalion or regiment
Nambokucho Period	1333–1392	tachi	relatively straight sword to be suspended horizontally from the left hip, preferred by mounted samurai
nimai-do	cuirass made of two parts (gomai-do: five parts)		
ninzoku, komono	baggage train attendant	taiko	drum
nobori, nobori no hata	large rectangular flag	taisho, -daisho	senior officer rank
nodawa	armoured throat protection, gorget	tatami-do	simple armour made of small iron plates sewn on cloth/leather
okashi gusoku	"borrowed" suits of armour supplied from the lord's arsenal	tate	shield, especially a large pavise
okegawa-do	cuirass composed of massive plates of iron, developed in the 16th c.	tate-eri	armoured shoulder protectors, introduced in the 16th c.
		teisatsu	spies, scouts
o-metsuke	battlefield analyst, chief of the metsuke / ikusa-metsuke	teppo, tanegashima	matchlock arquebus (since the 1540's)
onida	supply and baggage train, "large baggage"	tosei-gusoku	"modern suits of armour" developed in the 16th c., reflecting European influences
o-yoroi	a large, box-like suit of armour from the Heian Period	tozama	"outer allies" (= vassal families not originally allied to a lord)
ronin	an unemployed samurai without a position with a lord	tsukai-ban	unit of mounted messengers and scouts
sake	rice wine or simply an alcoholic drink	uma-jirushi	a senior commander's personal standard
samurai-daisho	commander of a field unit, a very senior position	umawari-shu	mounted life guards, elite samurai cavalry
sashimono	small flag or object fixed to the back of a suit of armour	wakizashi	short sword
Sengoku Period	„Age of the Country at War", 1467 to roughly 1600	yabusame	ritual mounted archery, performed in Shinto shrines
shikoro	neck protector attached to a helmet	yari	a lance for cutting and thrusting
		yodarekake	a suspended throat protector
shinrui	blood relatives	yoriki, keigo yoriki	junior officer, generally a mounted samurai
shinzan-shu	recently acquired bands of bands of vassals		
shogun	samurai generalissimo, ruler of Japan 1192–1867	yumi	bow
-shu	group, unit, contingent	yusei, yugur	flexible response unit
sodaisho	general	zengun, senzeigun	vanguard
sogo-nari kabuto	helmet with decorations resembling human hair	zunari-kabuto, hineno-kabuto	a helmet made of 5 or 3 steel parts, very common in the Sengoku Period

BIBLIOGRAPHY

Absolon, Trevor: *Samurai Armour: Volume I: The Japanese Cuirass.* Oxford: Osprey 2017.

Alte japanische Waffen. Aufsätze aus den Mitteilungen der Deutschen Gesellschaft für Natur- und Völkerkunde Ostasiens der Jahre 1884 bis 1908. Ed. by Wolfgang Ettig. Schmitten/Ts.: Tengu (Verlag W. Ettig) 2005.

Berry, Mary Elizabeth: *Hideyoshi.* Harvard University Press, new ed. 1989.

Bottomley, I. & A.P. Hopson: *Arms and Armor of the Samurai: The History of Weaponry in Ancient Japan.* Wingdale: Crescent Books 1988.

Bryant, J. A.: *Sekigahara 1600: Final Struggle for Power.* Oxford: Osprey 1999.

The Cambridge History of Japan. Vol. 3: *Medieval Japan.* Ed. by Kozo Yamamura. Cambridge 1990; Vol. 4: *Early Modern Japan.* Ed. by John Whitney Hall. Cambridge 1991.

Charney, Michael W.: *Southeast Asian Warfare 1300-1900.* Leiden, Boston: Brill 2004.

Conlan, Thomas: *Weapons & Fighting Techniques of the Samurai Warrior.* London: Amber Books 2008.

Cummins, Anthony & Minami, Yoshie: *Samurai War Stories: Teachings and Tales of Samurai Warfare.* The History Press Ltd. 2013. (English translation of, among others, Zohyo Monogatari)

Cummins, Anthony & Minami, Yoshie: *Samurai Arms, Armour & the Tactics of Warfare: The Collected Scrolls of Natori-Ryu.* London: Watkins Publishing 2018.

Cunningham, Don: *Samurai Weapons. Tools of the Warrior.* Rutland, Tokyo: Tuttle reprinted 2016.

Daruma. Japanese Art and Antiques Magazine: *Jingasa (Soldier's Caps)* No.27, pp. 32-44; *Armour for Foot Soldiers (Ashigaru)* (No.36, pp. 45–53); *Flat Jingasa* (No.42, pp. 44-52); *Atypical Jingasa* (No.57, pp. 40-52).

Date Masamune (= Rekishi Gunzo Series 19). Tokyo. Gakken 12th edition 1998.

Deutsches Klingenmuseum Solingen: *Die Kunst der Samurai. Erstes europäisches Symposium.* Köln 1984.

Frois, Luis: *Die Geschichte Japans (1549-1578).* Translated by G. Schurhammer & E.A. Voretzsch. Leipzig 1926.

Frois, Luis: *Kulturgegensätze Europa-Japan.* Monumenta Nipponica 15. Ed. by J.F. Schütte. Tokyo 1955.

Hall, John W., Nagahara, Keiji & Yamamura, Kozo (ed.): *Japan before Tokugawa. Political Consolidation and Economic Growth, 1500 to 1650.* Princeton University Press 1981.

Hawley, William M.: *Mon. The Japanese Family Crest.* Hollywood: Hawley, 2nd ed. 1976.

Ii, Tatsuo: *Aka zonae. Takeda to Ii to Sanada to.* Kyoto: Miyabi 2007.

Illustrated London News. August 17, 1861.

Isawa, Shoji (ed.): *Sengoku kachu-shu.* Tokyo: Gakken 2002.

Jansen, Marius B.: *Tosa in the Sixteenth Century: The 100 Article Code of Chosokabe Motochika.* In: John W. Hall/Marius B. Jansen, Studies in the Institutional History of Early Modern Japan. Princeton 1968, pp. 89-114.

Kure, Mitsuo: *Samurai. An Illustrated History.* Rutland, Tokyo: Tuttle 2002.

Lamers, Jeroen P.: *Japonicus Tyrannus. The Japanese Warlord Nobunaga Reconsidered* (= Japonica Nederlandica 8). Leiden: Hotei Publishing 2000.

Motoyama, Kazuki: *Kuroda Gundan. Josui, Nagamasa to 24-ki no Gyukaku Mushatachi.* Kyoto: Miyabi 2008.

Perrin, Noel: *Giving Up the Gun: Japan's Reversion to the Sword, 1543-1879.* Boston, Mass.: David R. Godine 1988, originally published in 1979.

Polenghi, Cesare: *Samurai of Ayutthaya. Yamada Nagamasa, Japanese Warrior and Merchant in Early Seventeenth Century Siam.* Bangkok: White Lotus 2009.

Pretzer, Xavid „Kiho" (ed. and translator): *O-umajirushi. A 17th-Century Compendium of Samurai Heraldry.* Cambridge, Massachusetts: The Academy of Four Directions 2015.

Ratti, Oscar & Westbrook, Adele: *Secrets of the Samurai. A Survey of the Martial Arts of Feudal Japan.* Rutland, Tokyo: Tuttle, 8th ed. 1996.

Samurai. Exhibition catalogue ed. by Historisches Museum der Pfalz Speyer. Ostfildern: Thorbecke 2008.

Sasama, Yoshihiko: *Ashigaru no Seikatsu.* Tokyo: Yuzankaku 1970.

Schwentker, Wolfgang: *Die Samurai.* München: Beck, 2nd ed. 2003.

Sengoku Kanto Sangokushi (= Rekishi Gunzo Series 2). Tokyo: Gakken, 2nd ed. 1994.

Sengoku Kassen Nyumon (= Rekishi Gunzo Archive 6). Tokyo: Gakken, 2008.

Senryaku Senjutsu Heiki (= Weapons, Strategy, Tactics 1). Tokyo. Gakken 1994.

Solum, Terje & Rue, Anders K.: *The Saga of the Samurai,* vols. 1-6. Garden Grove: Brookhurst Press 2003-2016.

Ströhl, Hugo Gerard: *Japanisches Wappenbuch – Nihon Moncho.* Schmitten/Ts.: Tengu (Verlag Wolfgang Ettig), New edition 2007.

Tanaka, Yoshiatsu: *Kiba Gundan.* In: Sengoku Kassen Taizen 1 (= Rekishi Gunzo Series 50), Tokyo 1997.

Totman, Conrad: *Tokugawa Ieyasu.* Torrance: Heian International 1983.

Tsukahara, Bokuden: *The Hundred Rules of War.* Translated by Eric Shahan. Createspace Independent Publishing Platform 2017.

Turnbull, Stephen: *The Lost Samurai: Japanese Mercenaries in South East Asia, 1593-1688.* Barnsley: Frontline Books 2021.

Turnbull, Stephen: *Samurai Armies 1467-1649.* Oxford: Osprey 2008.

Turnbull, Stephen: *The Samurai Warfare Sourcebook.* London: Arms and Armour Press 1998.

Turnbull, Stephen: *Samurai Warfare.* London: Arms and Armour Press 1996.

Turnbull, Stephen: *Samurai Warlords. The Book of the Daimyo.* London: Blandford Press 1989.

Vaporis, Constantine Nomikos: Samurai. *An Encyclopedia of Japan's Cultured Warriors.* Santa Barbara: ABC-CLIO 2019.

Weber, Till: Berlin: *Samurai Armies of the Late Sengoku Period. Volume II: Castles and Sieges, Artillery, Heraldry & Clothing.* Zeughaus 2022.

Yamamoto Kansuke: *The Sword Scroll (Gunpo Heiho Ki).* Translated by Eric Shahan et al. CreateSpace Independent Publishing Platform 2016.

Yoshikawa, Eiji: *Taiko: An Epic Novel of War and Glory in Feudal Japan.* Kodansha America 2011.

Zöllner, Reinhard: *Die Ludowinger und die Takeda. Feudale Herrschaft in Thüringen und Kai-no-kuni.* Bonn: Born 1995.

Zusetsu. Sengoku busho 118. Tokyo: Gakken 2001.

Zusetsu. Sengoku kassen-shu. Tokyo: Gakken 2001.

Selected Internet Resources in English

www.samurai-archives.com (close to 8000 articles on numerous aspects of the world samurai lived in)

https://sengokudaimyo.com/ (the late Anthony J. Bryant's website)

http://gunbai-militaryhistory.blogspot.com/2018/03/sengoku-period-warfare-part-1-army-and.html (a large collection of articles on Sengoku military history)

https://jref.com/articles/yamada-nagamasa.53/ (on Yamada Nagamasa)

https://jcastle.info/view/Home (aiming to be the most comprehensive site in English on Japanese castles)

http://www.samuraibookshop.com/ (Online source for the 1708 handbook Gunyo Senkou Zukai and other important source materials)

http://dl.ndl.go.jp/info:ndljp/pid/1287803/8 (the original O-Umajirushi heraldic scroll published online by the Japanese Diet Library)

https://www.touken-world.jp/search-flag/ (recommended site with many examples of Sengoku banners)

https://ukiyo-e.org/ (a useful site to search for woodblock prints including depictions of historical topics)

https://japanesword.com/ (excellent material on swords)

https://www.iz2.or.jp/english/ (The Costume Museum of Kyoto)

https://sengokujidai.org/ (based on William Barthell's skillful translations from the Japanese, still growing)

https://www.stephenturnbull.com/ (Website of the West's leading scholar of Things Samurai with dozens of publications in the field)

Photos by Till Weber

Tsukai-ban Mounted Messenger from Tokugawa Ieyasu's HQ

This elite samurai's sashimono back flag is emblazoned with the go character (= five), marking the man as a member of Ieyasu's *tsukai-ban* corps. In addition, he has a large red *horo* fixed to his back. This was an archaic item marking a distin- guished samurai, arguably also of some use against arrows and even arquebus balls fired at the horseman from behind. Basically, a *horo* is a bag made of silk or other fabrics and mounted on a light-weight bamboo or wicker frame. The bag would fill up with air when riding, giving it its balloon-like shape.

Samurai Armies of the Late Sengoku Period

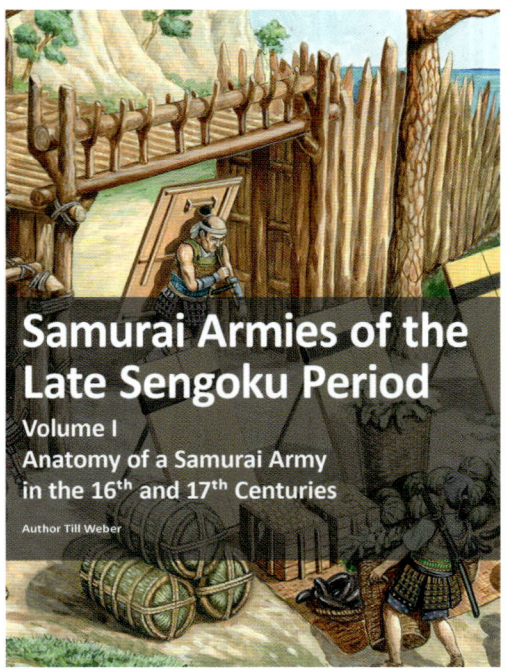

Volume I
Anatomy of a Samurai Army in the 16th and 17th Centuries

The „Anatomy of a samurai army" details its composition, hierarchies, strengths and weaknesses as well as examining how it fought. Other aspects include:
- the differences between samurai and European warfare;
- the roles assigned to samurai and ashigaru in different armies;
- how these armies, some of which were over 100,000 strong, functioned;
- marching orders and camp facilities of the armies and;
- where each individual samurai stood in the order of battle.

The reader will discover what may seem to be abstract or strange ideas by way of the most detailed examples possible, in both word and picture, that are based on a variety of Japanese sources.
104 pages.
ISBN 978-3-96360-041-8

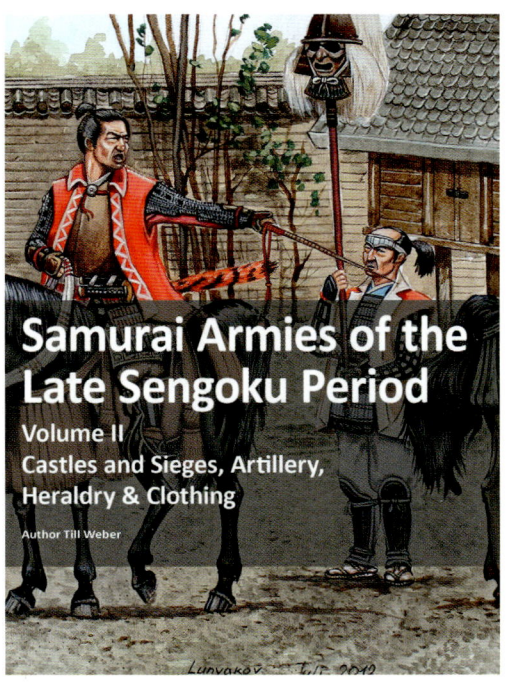

Volume II
Castles and Sieges, Artillery, Heraldry & Clothing

The elegant, multi-storey main towers of Japanese castles, surrounded by massive fortifications, are widely known as symbols of samurai rule. However, the first of these tenshukaku were built only at the very end of the Sengoku period. Most fortifications were built of wood with eart- hen ramparts and ditches exploiting the natural environment.

The second volume of this series details these constructions as well as the fortifications that were affected by major sieges: Fushimi, Tanabe, Otsu and Ueda in 1600, and Osaka in 1614/15. The author explains the sophisticated siege techniques and countermeasures employed by samurai armies of the period, and the Japanese artillery of the time.

A second focus is on the complex heraldry of leading as well as lesser known samurai families of the Sengoku period, illustrated by many colourful examples.

The third part offers an introduction to the world of traditional Japanese textile patterns and colours, their use, methods of manufacture in the pre-industrial age, and their special symbolism in the context of samurai history.

112 pages.
ISBN 978-3-96360-042-5

The books can be ordered online and are available at many bookstores.